KILLER POKER *NO LIMIT!*

KILLER POKER
NO LIMIT!

A Winning Strategy for
Cash Games and Tournaments

John Vorhaus

Kensington Publishing Corp.
www.kensingtonbooks.com

LYLE STUART BOOKS are published by

Kensington Publishing Corp.
850 Third Avenue
New York, NY 10022

All Kensington titles, imprints, and distributed lines are available at special quantity discounts for bulk purchases for sales promotions, premiums, fund-raising, educational, or institutional use. Special book excerpts or customized printings can also be created to fit specific needs. For details, write or phone the office of the Kensington special sales manager: Kensington Publishing Corp., 850 Third Avenue, New York, NY 10022, attn: Special Sales Department; phone 1-800-221-2647.

Lyle Stuart is a trademark of Kensington Publishing Corp.

First printing: March 2007

10 9 8 7 6 5 4 3 2 1

Printed in the United States of America

ISBN-13: 978-0-8184-0662-1
ISBN-10: 0-8184-0662-3

To my dad.

Contents

PART III: TOURNAMENT WONDERLAND

PART IV: SCRAPMETAL AND DOUGHNUTS

Foreword
by Mark Seif

It's been a hectic eight weeks. Just over seven weeks ago, my first child, Sarah, was born. Between playing poker full-time, working on the Professional Poker Tour, working with Absolute Poker, appearing at poker boot camps and fantasy camps, working on a host of other projects, and dealing with Sarah's reluctance to sleep more than ninety straight minutes, I have found little time to do "other things." The writing of this foreword was one of those other things. Finally, now I can do it and I am really pleased to do so because I have something good to share with you. It's really John Vorhaus who is sharing it with you, but I can take credit for recommending it. It's this book. It's chock-full of good stuff that *will* help your no-limit game. It's that simple.

Just before Sarah was born I was contacted by my friend, John Vorhaus. We talked about various things, including my wife Jennifer's pregnancy and the impending birth of our daughter, and John also mentioned that he had just completed a new book, *Killer Poker No Limit!* ("KPNL"). I was happy to hear about KPNL because I had read a couple of John's other books and have always found some pearls of wisdom that I was able to incorporate into my game—and sometimes into my life. When John then offered to send me the manuscript and have me write the foreword to it if I was so inclined, I happily accepted the offer and was flattered as well.

So, a little while later I received the KPNL manuscript via e-mail. Knowing that it's not a good idea to try to read more than a couple of pages onscreen, I decided to print it out on my killer new all-in-everything printer. (And isn't it amazing how cheap these things are now? But I digress.) Before I printed out KPNL, I decided to take a look at how many pages this job would be. I thought that KPNL would be like John's other books—a cozy, handbook type of read. I was quite surprised to find that this baby was nearly 300 pages! So, I put off printing it until I had more time and a spare ink cartridge.

Between the time John sent me the manuscript and the time I actually got around to printing it, I had occasion to talk to him about another poker-related subject. Somehow we got on the topics of playing, teaching, writing about poker, etc.—stuff you would expect two guys like us to talk about. Naturally, we started talking about the KPNL manuscript, which I had not yet read, of course. John mentioned that in KPNL he claims that whoever has the most fun wins. To which I responded, "Are you kidding me? Most fun wins?!" I told John that I make it a point to start off each one of my Boot Camp seminars by drawing the important difference between fun/social poker and the other type of poker—namely, the kind of poker that wins world championships and millions of dollars. In fun/social poker, I point out that one might win or lose a palatable amount, but generally have a good time either way.

Then there's the type of poker I call "eat their children" poker, a phrase I borrowed from that famous Mike Tyson prefight interview, where he said in his high-pitched girlie voice, "I wanna eat his children." While that was clearly a crude, wildly barbaric remark, it always sends a chill down my spine, because Mike Tyson wants to do the worst possible thing to his opponents—eat their children—and that's *exactly* what I and every other top-level pro want to do to our opponents at the poker table: the worst possible thing. Within, of course (and unlike Mike), the rules of civilized social behavior. *Wow,* I thought, *so John and I fundamentally disagree on the basic approach to poker. He wants to have fun and I want to commit virtual crimes! Well, John's a good friend and I at least should read the book. Give it a shot and see what happens.*

So I started reading KPNL. One thing I fondly experienced again was John's terrific writing style. He's a powerful writer who has the ability to actually write the way he talks. It's refreshing and easy to follow. His words are easily digestible but they have substance—meaning. John even does this with concepts as dry as poker math. John also stays true to form in KPNL in the "lists" department. All of his books I've read require you to do a type of self-analysis, game-analysis, soul-searching, inventory-taking, list-making exercise, revealing to yourself the good, the bad, and the ugly about your poker game. I think the vast majority of serious poker players never do this. John almost matter-of-factly discusses serious and troubling holes in his game and makes it easy—or should I say, easier, for you to find the same or different holes in your game. It's almost like going to group therapy where someone admits that they are not a perfect poker player at all times and then you admit the same thing. Then you move on to the next eleven steps until you are all better. I find this type of exercise extremely helpful to my game and to my life in general, but never easy. Indeed, very few motivators have inspired me to do these difficult self-exploratory tasks. John does it here.

I really liked what this book was making me do right from the start, but in the back of my mind I still wondered how John and I were going to resolve our fundamental differences. I also wondered if he'd gone soft. After all, John's earlier Killer Poker books inspired (indeed, incited) us to overpower, overwhelm, dominate, beat and crush our opponents. Now, that was consistent with my personal philosophy and style of play. So what was with this have the most fun stuff?

Suspending disbelief, I read on. I was soon quite surprised and pleased to learn that John's definition of "most fun" is virtually identical to my call for eating your opponents' children. Within the first twenty pages of KPNL, John comes out with the bridge, the connection, the union between our two divergent takes. And it's good. John states, "I propose that we simply redefine fun in no limit hold'em as knowing what's the right thing to do and then doing it. Let's just let performing well be our biggest kick, and gauge our enjoyment according to this handy math: Good Play = Good Fun, Better Play = More Fun, Best Play = Most Fun and most fun wins." Ahh . . . John *does* get it! I was doubly pleased by this discovery because now I could throw myself into John's take on no-limit hold'em and therefore have a chance to take my game up a notch by incorporating some of his concepts into the principle that I have long advanced (and happily found that he did not refute). Can we call this "Have fun by eating their children?" I don't see why not.

So, what can you expect from KPNL? You can expect KPNL to challenge you to analyze your strengths, weaknesses, style, and how you see yourself in the game. Then you can expect a logical discussion about how your aversion or affinity to risk influences and even dictates how you play. What I really enjoyed were the specific questions and fact patterns that John uses to determine types of players. John takes us through a detailed analysis of being risk averse versus risk affined and there are pearls of wisdom as to the need for striking the perfect balance. This is really good stuff, and John provides a multitude of real-life examples to illustrate how risk affinity, or the lack thereof, factors into virtually every decision we and our opponents make.

In another section, John talks about the need to have a plan for the hand; this, too, is powerful stuff. One of the factors that distinguishes the best poker players in the world from the merely good ones is the crafty, specific, strategic analysis and execution they bring to every hand they play. In other words, the best players often pump a ton of thought into critical situations, while most others seem to act based on experience, intuition, and often minimal insight. A good plan at the outset of the hand could mean the difference between tremendous success and utter failure. This, too, I have learned.

KPNL states that we need to be unpredictable and inconsistent at the table. Again, this is a fundamental truth. I like John's approach here and he is careful to caution us against the pitfalls of such play. I also really enjoyed the section titled "A Good Day at Play," where John states, "Because no limit hold'em is such an unforgiving game, we need to be ready to win every time we sit down to play, for errors that cost us a big bet or two in a limit hold'em cash game will take us off our whole stack in no limit." This should be self-evident, but for many players it is not, and John even provides a nice checklist of what you need before you sit down to play a no limit session. Since such needs inevitably include money, John discusses bankroll requirements for buying in to a no limit cash game. While his guidelines are fundamentally sound, this is one poker player who always prefers to buy in big. In my view, I find it much more difficult to sleep at night knowing that I didn't put enough money on the table to take full advantage of an opponent's mistake. Plus, my ultra loose/aggressive playing style simply demands it.

In his section on tournament play, John offers measurably profitable advice about the early, middle, and late stages of a tournament, and how one's strategy must adjust accordingly. In today's poker world, where winning a major tournament can bring you a ton of fame and fortune, you will spend your time wisely by reading and re-reading this section if you plan on playing in any serious tournaments. There's no doubt, in my view, that great tournament strategy is more important than great poker strategy when it comes to winning poker tournaments. KPNL speaks volumes on this subject.

In sum, then, it gives me great pleasure to recommend this book. I think you will find it most fun for yourself and most deadly to your foes. Simply put, KPNL forces us to examine our game (and in some cases ourselves) in ways previously known by only a tiny fraction of poker players. Let the games begin!

MARK SEIF *stunned the poker world by winning back-to-back events at the 2005 World Series of Poker. As a teacher at the WPT Boot Camp and other poker fantasy camps, Mark provides poker concepts and teaching techniques that have helped thousands win millions.*

Acknowledgments

There's this guy I want to thank. I don't know his name, but he sat across from me in a no limit hold'em game about four months ago at the Bicycle Casino. I was in a serious funk about this book; it was being frustratingly slow to show me its shape and substance. And so I did what I do when the work daunts me: I quit for the day and went to play poker. I thought the break would clear my head, or perhaps give me some key insight to help me get unstuck. Well, this guy recognizes me and says, "Hey, you're that Killer Poker guy!" He effuses for a moment or two, which I admit I never hate, but then he says something that hits me like a two-by-four.

"What I like about your books," he said, "is you remind me that poker's supposed to be fun."

And he thanked me for that.

And I thank him for that. For reminding me what I know to be true, that poker is supposed to be fun. I've tried to endow this book with that spirit, and it's a surprising point of view for a poker book, I suppose, but if all we ever think about is the money, then where's the enjoyment? And if there's no enjoyment then what, really, is the point?

Beyond this anonymous patron, I need to thank my brain trust, Tony Guerrera and Craig Vieregg, for helping me think things through; for fixing my math; for challenging my assumptions; and for busting my ego where necessary. Thanks to Annie Duke for giving me the very simple 411 on tournament dealmaking. Thanks to Greg Dinkin and Frank Scatoni at Venture Literary for being the last agents I'll ever need. Thanks to Richard Ember, my editor extraordinaire. Thanks to Mark Seif for classing up the joint.

Thanks to Maxx, always to Maxx. She rocks my world.

Introduction:
MOST FUN WINS

I'm just sitting here this morning musing on the nature of addiction. I certainly have my share of addictions spread out around me. At my left hand is a mug filled with hot coffee, to which I am addicted. It's not just any mug, either, but my *Comic Toolbox* promotional mug, which I've been addicted to drinking from ever since I wrote the book of the same name. I know it's just subjective reality, but I swear the coffee tastes better in that mug. At my right hand is the sudoku from this morning's paper. Sudoku has lately replaced crosswords as my number-one puzzle addiction. And puzzles are a *sick* addiction for me. I swear I could do life behind bars if I had enough acrostics and scanagrams. My mind hates to be idle. Believe me when I tell you that I can't even stand to stand in a super-market checkout line without something to read, even if it's only a *National Enquirer* headline. ("Angry Trucker Fires Five Shots Into UFO!") Among other things, I am addicted to the written word.

Among other things. So many other things. Before me sits my computer screen, which pushes addictions like email, blogs, weather maps, baseball stats, information streams of all sorts. Music is playing on the radio. Jazz. Lately I've been addicted to jazz. Looking out my window, I see the postman approaching,

1

so I know that now I have to drop everything, because I'm addicted to the mail and its promise of exciting personal correspondence and expected—or unexpected—paychecks, though I know I'll probably just be disappointed by the usual deluge of catalogs, coupon books, and come-ons for credit cards. Now my dog trots into the room. He's addicted to having his head scratched, and I'm addicted to scratching it. We're codependents in this. Since he's also addicted to chasing squirrels, he will gladly join me later when I go out to run in the park. I'm not addicted to running, but I am addicted to endorphins and you get those by running, so that's that with that.

I could easily continue listing my addictions (for I'm also addicted to lists) but I think you get the point. I'm hooked on many things. Nor am I alone in this. We all have our hooking points: favorite sports team; favorite food or drink; hobbies; shops; friends; lovers; family; philosophy; and on and on and on. In a moment I'm going to ask you what you're hooked on, but before I do, let me tell you why I raise the subject in the first place. You see, I just finished writing a book on poker, *Killer Poker Online/2*. Having delivered the manuscript, I told myself that I should knock off for a while and let my batteries recharge before I started my next book on poker, this book on poker. I told myself I deserved a vacation, and I do. But what is a workaholic's holiday except more work? If I'm addicted to anything, I'm addicted to writing, and so my resolve to just . . . not . . . write . . . lasted a grand total of three days. I got antsy. I got the sweats. I washed the windows, and then I washed them again. I even watched daytime TV. It was not pretty. So I withdrew from withdrawal and got back to work . . . back to my number one hooking point. I couldn't stay away, and I can't stay away, and this is not a good thing or a bad thing, but just a thing I own.

What can't you stay away from? Setting aside the question of whether these are good things or bad things, for value judgments are not the point of this exercise, please list your top ten pastimes, passions, or obsessions—your hooking points, if you will. I assume that poker is somewhere on that list, because otherwise why would you have fallen into this book? But where on the list do you place it? Above or below family? Above or below exercise? Above or below (or alongside) that smoky Laphroaig single malt? If poker is number one, that's fine. If it's number ten, that's fine, too. Again, this isn't about value judgments. I'm just interested in knowing—well, in having you know—the main activities that float your boat.

>>

(Those who know my books know that the >> symbol means *write your answer here or elsewhere*. Those who didn't know that before know it now.)

I don't ask this question in order to pry into your private life, but rather to invite *you* to pry into your private life, because in poker as in, say, piloting a helicopter, what you don't know can hurt you.

Consider Sugar Dave.

Sugar Dave is a no limit hold'em (NLHE) player I know and let me tell you, he's the real deal: He's aggressive, fearless, and canny, and he senses weakness the way sharks smell blood. He's especially gifted in tournaments, where these days he does quite well. Such wasn't always the case, though. See, Dave was hooked on sweets (hence the nickname) and he often hit the snack bar or gift shop during tournament breaks, loading up on doughnuts or Dove bars or candy. Trouble was, sugar made him nuts. Jacked up on the stuff, he'd return to the tournament table, bet himself way out ahead of his hands, and bust out explosively. It sounds far-fetched I know, but it's true, and it wasn't until Sugar Dave changed his diet (and his name to Aspartame Dave) that he became the tournament stud he nowadays is.

Sugar Dave, then, had a hooking point that worked at cross-purposes to profit in poker. Such hooking points abound. Alcohol is a notorious example. Drugs are another. Many top players are known to leak their winnings away through other forms of gambling like blackjack or craps. Being a sucker for sudoku, I used to try to multitask—multirecreate?—at the poker table by working a sudoku between hands. Of course this slayed my attention and killed my prospects for profit, so I broke myself of the habit. How about you? Revisiting your list of hooking points above, can you see any that might hurt your poker play?

>>

If you have trouble frankly admitting these things, trust me—you're in abundant company. But consider that the more honest you are, the better your poker play will become; therefore you can use self-interest (the goal of winning more money) to defeat self-protection (the fear of facing facts) and let your passion for profit trump your natural reluctance to tell the truth about you to you. This is a practical path to self-awareness, one with no loftier ambition than to play better poker. Studying ourselves, then, examining ourselves in the unflinching light of reality, we discover a tangled web of connections between our hooking points and our poker play. Nor is this news, for poker performance is affected by everything from eating habits and physical health to philosophical bent and family relationships. We also discover—we, the writer and the readers of this book—that one of our greatest hooking points is, hey, *poker itself.* Again, not news. I'm hooked on poker. You're hooked on poker. Pretty much everyone who plays the game gets hooked to one degree or another. It's that compelling.

Seriously, do you know anyone who started playing poker and then stopped?

Me neither.

Personally, I find poker to be a pretty positive addiction. It provides me with a social framework, keeps my mind sharp (gives me something to write about), and—if I'm doing it right— puts money in my pocket. I could certainly see someone arguing the other side, though, that poker is a dangerous degeneracy that smart people would hold at arm's length. And some smart people *do* hold it at arm's length. I have one friend who's so keenly interested in poker that he goes out of his way to avoid learning anything about it. "I can get addicted to anything I become aware of," he says, and so keeps himself unschooled in the game.

It is, of course, increasingly hard to stay unschooled about poker, since poker thrusts itself these days upon even the most casual channel surfer, magazine rack browser, or cocktail party conversationalist. Billboards for online poker sites abound. Poker chip sets are sold everywhere from Home Depot to Pottery Barn. I've seen my own books for sale in airport bookstores and the back racks at Costco. Poker is huge, poker is hot, and poker is here to stay.

Once again, not news. So not news.

So what do we do with it? What do we do with the teeming multitudes of newly minted poker players chasing their newfound buzz across the fuzzy green felt of Las Vegas casinos, traipsing into local cardrooms in record numbers, or clogging the lobbies of online poker sites? Why, take their money, of course. Not that they'll give it up without a fight. The poker population is trending new, true, but it's not a completely clueless parade. There are plenty of quick learners out there, plus tested veterans who were poker when poker wasn't cool. And they all have their eye on our money as much as we have our eye on theirs. So we take their measure. Devise strategies to beat them. Pit our skills against their skills, our guts against theirs. We match our ability to solve the puzzle of them against their ability to solve the puzzle of us. We avoid the strong ones, attack the weak ones, and, if all goes according to plan, leave with our bankrolls choked with their Franklins and our throats choked with the satisfaction of a job well done.

And we do this all in the context of virtually the only poker game that anybody plays these days: no limit Texas hold'em, "the Cadillac of poker," as famously described by Doyle Brunson.

It was a Cadillac almost no one cared to drive during the gradual growth of poker's popularity, from 1987, when flop games became legal in California, until 2003 and the WPT/Moneymaker revolution. Limit hold'em was long the structure of choice because even the worst players went broke slowly enough to stay in the action and keep the games going. NLHE, the purview of leather assed rounders with fat wallets and long experience, tended to bust new players too quickly, like a maladaptive virus that prematurely kills the host body. Not to put too fine a point on it, NLHE was too expensive a game to play badly, and almost everyone plays badly at first.

But now here comes the World Poker Tour and here comes internet poker, with the former provoking the itch to play no limit and the latter providing a place to scratch. On the level playing field of *we're all figuring this out as we go along*, low buy in NLHE games quickly began to flourish online. From there they backdoored into the realworld cardrooms, putting the squeeze on such formerly popular poker variants as limit hold'em, seven-card stud, and Omaha. The cardrooms, good adaptors not at all interested in killing the host body, spread the game with low blinds and, crucially, capped buy-ins. These conventions proved an effective brake on new players' losses, as did the advent of low buy in NLHE tournaments. Mostly, though, it was the flood tide of new players, all equally (in)experienced, whose overwhelming numbers guaranteed that money put in play would stay in play, in the hands of players not particularly adept at holding on to it. NLHE, the former purview of leather assed rounders, had become the game of choice for entry level players. And the rush, as they say, was on.

It's a funny thing about NLHE, a thing that sets it apart from limit. No matter how small their stacks are, most players are quite passionate about defending them. You can be playing NLHE for $25 or $5 or even no dollars at all, and you still want to win. To go all in and double up is a thrill beyond words. To go all in and lose is a chilling nightmare. And this steep roller-coaster ride, from elation to desolation and back, is a thrill that limit poker just can't match. Play $1–$2 limit hold'em, where an unraised pot will cost you just six bucks between here and the river, and it's hard to give a rat's ass. Play NLHE with $1–$2 blinds, where one wrong move can take them (or you) off the stack they (or you) have worked for hours to build, and it's hard to keep the shakes at bay. That's the buzz of poker, distilled down to its purest form and mainlined every day by millions of NLHE aficionados worldwide. That's why everyone these days plays no limit.

That's why you and I probably play, too, if we're honest enough to admit it. Sure we want profit. Sure we want to dominate and crush. We may even have dreams of playing poker professionally, or scaling the heights of televised poker stardom, but—again, if we're honest—we have to admit that our passion for poker begins with the buzz. Many people fight against this admission. They claim to approach the game with dispassionate detachment, denying that the highs (and lows) of poker affect them in any way. I consider this to be a useful fiction, a bit of propaganda they lay upon themselves to maintain an even keel. There's nothing wrong with such self-manipulation, for a fiction may be fiction but useful just the same. Also, though, it's *fiction* . . . a lie, and no poker player can hope to prosper with lies flying around in her head.

(Author's note: In my last book, when third person pronouns were called for, I used the male: he/him/his. This time, in the name of fairness and all, I'm going to mix it up. While most poker players are yet male, it's a changing world and a changing poker demographic, so I will ask you to cut me some slack on this. In the name of fairness and all.)

Why don't we all just admit that we *love to play poker*? We can call it a hobby or a pastime or a passion if that soothes us. Or we can call it an obsession or addiction if we're strong enough to own the truth. But whatever we call it, let's recognize it for what it is: a delight that trumps many other delights in our lives.

Go to the movies or go play poker?

> *Poker.*

Go to a party or go to Party Poker?

> *Well, the games are pretty good there now.*

Go to the gym or go to the club?

> *Can't make money at the gym!*

And so it goes, and so we all go, in relentless pursuit of poker profit but poker pleasure, too. Can you see how these two fundamental hooking points might clash? Can you think of poker mistakes you might make if you thought you were only in it for the money but were actually in it for the fun as well?

>>

I can think of a few. Absent pure clarity of purpose, I'd likely

- play poker when I'm not mentally prepared
- play too many hands
- make self-indulgent tricky plays
- get involved in reckless adventures
- get in games I can't beat

So how do we achieve clarity of purpose? Through staunch denial of poker's buzz? That's an approach, I suppose. With a schoolmarm's sternness we could admonish ourselves, "You're here to make money, not here to have fun!" And every time we catch ourselves having fun we could whap our own knuckles with a ruler. Would that work? Would that trend us toward perfect poker, or just leave us stuck in a joyless exercise where, yeah, we might make money, but to what end and at what cost? Turning ourselves into poker automatons, we might very well triumph but would never relish the win.

We might try going the other way. We might say, "Screw the money, I'm just here to have fun." Following that line of logic, we'd play more hands, see more flops, take more draws, make more bets, and have a really good time playing really bad poker. Of course, the inevitable consequence of playing bad poker is losing lots of money. Maybe so much money that we can no longer afford to stay in the game. Fun over. Next case.

I propose a third path, one that neither kills the kick of poker nor moves us off appropriate discipline. I propose that we simply redefine fun in no limit hold'em as knowing what's the right thing to do and then doing it. Let's just let performing well be our biggest kick and gauge our enjoyment according to this handy math:

GOOD PLAY = GOOD FUN
BETTER PLAY = MORE FUN
BEST PLAY = MOST FUN

AND MOST FUN WINS.

Lay down pocket kings when there's an ace on board and much betting? Fun. Fold pocket jacks preflop in the face of a raise, a reraise, and a call? Fun. Bet a scare card on the turn and get 'em to fold? Fun. Pick off a bluff from a crazy raiser? Fun! Fold J-3, T-2, K-4, 6-9, 7-2, 7-4, 8-5? Fun, fun, fun, fun, fun, fun, FUN!

This strategy starts by acknowledging the truth: that we want to play winning poker, but we also want to relish the rush. Then it simply redefines fun, and in so doing gives us a way to link these two hooking points in a powerful common cause. Now we get to have all the fun we want. By playing perfect poker. It's not a goal we're likely to achieve anytime soon. Hell, it's not a goal we're likely to achieve anytime ever. But if poker is your joy, as it is mine, you want to leverage your skill as far as possible in pursuit of that joy. Every time you find yourself making the right move for the right reason against the right foe—whether you get the right result or not—you get to reward yourself with the deep and profound satisfaction of a job well done. And that, if you let it, will be the biggest buzz of all.

So what do you say, folks? Shall we all go have some fun?

PART I

♣♠♦♥

US AND THEM

1

HOW GREEN IS MY WALLY?

The first thing to consider about no limit hold'em (NLHE) is how many hundreds (thousands? hundreds of thousands?) of people are coming into the game each day completely ill-equipped to play it correctly. Driven to a frenzy of enthusiasm by televised poker—now airing on every channel but Disney and the Home Shopping Network—inspired by dreams of easy money, and seduced by the ready availability of the online game, these Johnny-(Chan)-come-latelies think that a couple of sitngos and a quick skim of *Super System 2* qualify them as rounders. They couldn't be more wrong—to the tune of pretty much every penny they put in play.

Right off the bat, then, you have to ask yourself if you have what it takes to go the distance. I'm not talking about money. Any jamoke with a day job can put together a bankroll. Nor am I talking about guts, though NLHE does challenge one's fortitude. No, what I'm talking about is ambition: the willingness to work hard in service of perfect poker. Simply put, if you won't bust your ass to play the game right, the game will bust your ass for you.

Let me show you what I mean.

A typical no limit newbie finds himself in Las Vegas for a haberdashers' convention. Late one night, his business done for the day, his intestines distended by a heavy meal, and his mind muddied by fine wine (or what passes for such in Vegas), he slopes into the poker room of the new and fabulous Insidion Hotel and Casino. Excited to try the game he's seen on TV and even played once or twice with friends in someone's rumpus room, he sits down at the first NLHE table he sees. This is of course a mistake in game selection, but game selection is yet to this pumpkin a concept as foreign as Zoroastrianism or the ancient mariner's art of macramé, so let's let that go for now.

A garden variety Wally (cally Wally; a weak, loose player), he fumbles his buy in a bit and eventually plunks down the table minimum. This is both good news and bad news for our Wally. Having bought in for the minimum, he stands to lose the least he can lose; however, having bought in for the minimum, he marks himself as either scared or green or both. He further reinforces his rookie image by immediately taking a hand under the gun (UTG), not waiting for his big blind or for the button to pass. He picks up pocket jacks, and blithely calls his way into the pot.

Waiting to act next is a cagey, experienced player we'll call Sandi Seabed. She studies him carefully. She can tell by the way Wally fumbled his buy in, by the way he handles his chips, by the way he didn't wait for the optimum time to jump in, and by his overall fretful demeanor that he's out of his element and depth. She makes a big raise, immediately putting Wally's feet to the fire. Wally doesn't much like that. He knows enough about hold'em to know that big pocket pairs are good cards, but not enough to know that—big pocket pairs notwithstanding—Sandi has a plan to outplay him on the flop. Further, he's not comfortable having to commit so many chips so early. Heck, his seat isn't even warm yet; his free drink hasn't even arrived.

But pocket jacks are pocket jacks, so Wally calls. The flop comes A-Q-3, and Wally is lost in the hand. Fearing those over-cards, he meekly checks. Of course, Sandi bets; she puts Wally all in. Poor Wally. He knows too little about card odds to judge whether it's likely that Sandi has an ace or a queen. And he knows *nothing* about his opponent, so he can't gauge whether she'd bluff here or not. All he knows is that if he calls here and loses, he'll have lost his entire buy in on the first hand. He will be *miserable*.

In the name of not being miserable, he folds.

In the name of messing with Wally's head, Sandi shows the 8♥-7♥ with which she drove him off the hand. Now Wally *really* feels lousy.

And his night just gets worse from there. Stung by the hurt and humiliation of having been bluffed off a big pot, desperate to ease the psychic pain he feels, Wally buys in again and immediately starts overplaying his hands. Soon he's hemorrhaging at the wallet, pouring buy in after buy in into the game until, finally financially flatlined, he staggers away from the table and stumbles off to find the other haberdashers or possibly a slot machine where even if he loses at least he won't feel so punked.

Now, at this point all Wally has going against him is lack of experience. To be fair, he probably doesn't know enough about NLHE to be aware of the many mistakes he's made, and that's fine. But if he comes back tomorrow night and the night after that and plays the same way, then that's not fine. If he thinks he lost by luck that first time—*those darn pocket jacks, why didn't they hold up?!*—and counts on luck to see him through the next time, then he's just compounding his mistakes and dooming himself to a long, unsatisfactory relationship with the game. He stands at a crossroads. He can either assign himself the task of learning the game properly or assign himself the role of permanent loser.

Not a pretty picture, eh? Not one I'd want for myself nor, I know, one you'd want for yourself. So let me ask you a question: Considering your level of knowledge and experience, are you at this moment closer to Wally or to Sandi in ability, aptitude, and approach to the game? If you care to amplify your answer, list the ways in which you're like each. (If you care to

amply your answer elsewhere, you'll find some blank lined
pages at the back of the book.)
    >>

If you have even a modest history in poker, you probably
consider yourself to be well past the sort of green gaffes a
Wally would make. And probably you are. But in fact you're
much closer to Wally than to Sandi—I am, we all are—for the
simple reason that Sandi doesn't actually exist. Wallies exist;
Wallies abound. But Sandi is an ideal, a paragon of poker who
plays powerfully and correctly hand after hand, hour after
hour, day after week after month after year. She's the end of
our rainbow, the goal we aspire to but will never attain. No
matter where we are in our poker journey, the first thing we
must do is acknowledge that we're much closer to the beginning than to the end, because the beginning is clear and present but the end remains, like the end of the rainbow, always
out of reach. That's not a problem, nor any cause for dismay
for, as Robert Browning said, "A man's reach should exceed his
grasp. Or what's a heaven for?" In other words,

IT'S PROCESS
NOT PRODUCT
THAT COUNTS.

If we're working hard and evolving in poker, it doesn't
matter how endless the road ahead may be. We're moving forward, growing in the game. That's all that matters. I like this
approach to growth, for while perfection is an unattainable
goal, improvement can be had every day. By constantly growing in poker we have reason to feel proud of our efforts even
when outcomes let us down. And while it may dismay you to
suffer bad beats with nothing but the cold comfort of "improvement" as solace, I put it to you that keeping your eyes on

this prize offers not just psychic benefits but cash ones as well. Every mistake you stop making puts money in your pocket in the long run—even if it didn't this time. Every edge you exploit increases your expected value—even if it didn't this time. Every situation you correctly analyze improves your bottom line—even if it didn't this time. Look past outcomes, then, and focus instead on the fundamental question: *Am I playing better now than I did before?* Good news: With this as your focus, you get the twin satisfactions of strengthening your play and of seeing tangible results from the changes you've made over time.

More good news: You *are* playing better now than you did before, and you can prove it to yourself through a simple test. Casting your mind back to when you started playing NLHE (whether last year or last week), take a moment and list ten things you do better now than then. Since ten is a large number, I'll generate my list first and invite you to borrow what's also true for you.

- Get correct odds for my drawing hands.
- Attack blinds with appropriate frequency.
- Play A-K with proper bold caution.
- Get away from dominated holdings.
- Leave games when I'm beat and can't compete.
- Track results religiously.
- Take bad beats in stride.
- Compute pot odds on the fly.
- Pay attention to tendencies and tells.
- Protect big pocket pairs.

Now you.
>>

Interesting, isn't it? By using the modest little tool of the list, we can peer back in time and accurately measure our present selves against who we once were. Even more interesting, by using this tool we can likewise peer into the future and measure our present selves against who we will become, for if we're better players today than we were yesterday (last week, last year) and if we're dedicated to a course of constant improvement and growth, then it stands to reason that we're not as good at the game now as we will be one day. With this in mind, please draw up a list of ten ways you predict your game will grow. As before, I'll go first; and no, I'm not trying to hog all the revelations, I'm just trying to model honesty. So here are ten things I'd like to (and plan to) do better than I do right now.

- Play A-Q correctly.
- Make good laydowns.
- Think before I act.
- Pick off bluffs.
- Play stronger.
- Never glower.
- Trust my reads.
- Know when I'm beat.
- Stop getting trapped.
- Improve my math and memory.

I am aware that some of the items on my list trigger a real twinge of regret, even recrimination. *You moron! Why do you still get stuck on A-Q?* I honor these feelings, because they're real, but I don't let them get me down. If this seems like a delicate dance, it is, but part of becoming a better player is mastering the art of simultaneously hanging on and letting go. We have to hang on to our mistakes long enough to learn from them, for to let go without learning is to put us in the pit of Santayana: "Those who cannot remember the past are condemned to repeat it." But when we're done learning, we have to let go; otherwise, we'll never play poker with confidence and joy, and even if we could play well without confidence and joy (an open question, that) we'd never play happy, and that would be sad.

So, with head held high, holding regret at bay, list ten things in poker you'll do better later than you do right now.

>>

Did anyone say anything about taking control of the table? Because that's something we could all stand to do more of, and something Sandi showed us how to do against Wally. Note that her method was measured, not maniacal. First she observed the several mistakes Wally made in entering the game. Then, based on available information, she formed a hypothesis: *I can take this green guy.* Next she made and executed the plan of raising his flat call and betting any flop. Finally, having gotten him to fold, she pushed his tilt button by showing her naked bluff. We could argue whether this reveal was sporting, or even strategically sound (since it betrayed something of her mind-set to others at the table) but there's no arguing that it achieved the desired result of making a bad player play even worse.

And yes, the hand could have gone the other way. Wally could have spiked a jack on the flop, or simply not believed that Sandi had him beat. Or his fumbly entrance into the game could have been image, an act. But we have to commend Sandi's play—and, folks, *emulate* Sandi's play—because she saw an opportunity and she seized it. The opportunity had little to do with the cards she held and much to do with the foe she faced. After all, against most opponents Sandi will fold that 8-7 suited, and that's the sensible thing to do. Against a rare few, she'll push all in because she knows they can't call. Against yet others, she'll just call along and hope to catch a trapping hand. In all events, Sandi is not playing just her cards. She's playing the intersection of her cards and her opponents. Where these streets meet . . .

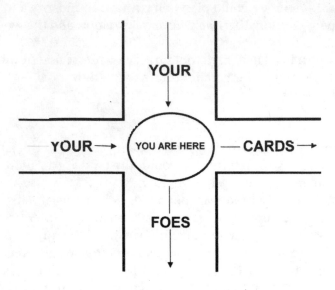

. . . is where quality poker lives.

Remember, your cards are only one source of available information. Your opponents are always streaming data at you, giving you important clues about how to defeat them. If they're weak and straightforward, you can use that. If they're tricky and creative, you can use that. If you've never played a single hand against them before, you can use that, too (because they've never played a hand against you, either). The Wallies of this world ask only, "How do I play these cards?" The Killer Poker player asks, "How do I play these cards *against these foes*?" It makes all the difference in the world.

Forget what you think you know about NLHE. Forget all your start charts and your odds computations. Well, all right, don't forget them, but set them aside for now. That information is useful, but it's only *half* useful because it doesn't put your cards in the context of the other players at the table. Sure, some hands play themselves: the hammer (2-7) gets folded; pocket aces get raised. But those hands are the ends of the spectrum. It's the hands in between hands, like 6-6, J-T suited, and my dreaded A-Q, that we have to know how to play correctly. And we can't know how to play them correctly unless we know who we're playing them against. What we need, then, is a quick and dirty system for parsing our foes reasonably accurately into categories.

I happen to have one here. . . .

2

"TYPE" CASTING

Multiple choice question:

In a $5–$10 blind no limit game, you're on the button hold-
ing K♠-9♠ and it's folded around to you. You have about
$1,000 in front of you, as do the small blind and the big
blind. Do you . . .

a. Fold?
b. Call?
c. Raise a little?
d. Raise a lot?

Some of you may declare shenanigans on this question, because didn't I just get done saying that you can't intelligently
attack the hand without knowing your foes? Okay, then, given
that the small blind is extremely loose and the big blind is extremely tight, tell me what you'll do—and, while you're at it,
why?

>>

Your answer to this question tells you a lot about the type
of player you are right now. If you could get all your foes to

answer this question truthfully, it would tell you a lot about them, too. Since they're not likely to be so genially forthcoming with such critical strategic information, you need to make deductions based upon their play, and then compile these deductions into some sort of unified picture of them. We'll get to that in a moment, but first let's get back to you, and the answer you just gave.

IF YOU FOLDED. If you folded this hand, you missed out on an opportunity to attack the blinds in favorable position with a better than average holding. Since the small blind is ultra loose and you expect him to call, it may be that you're just not looking for a fight, even though there's a good chance you'll be going to war with the best hand. There's nothing wrong with folding here, especially if you don't trust your postflop play, but it's not what you'd call a bold choice, so let's classify you as *wary*.

IF YOU CALLED. There are two reasons for calling here. Either you feel you can extract extra value from your out-of-position foes after the flop or you're just timid. The trouble with, essentially, slow playing an only okay hand is that the small blind will call with anything and the big blind gets a free ride with a random hand, so you won't know where you're at on the flop, and you'll probably need to hit to win. Since the strategy for flat calling is thus problematic, we'll characterize this play as *lax*.

IF YOU RAISED A LITTLE. This is the standard blind steal in a standard blind stealing situation. It's not particularly creative, but it is effective, as it invites the small blind to err on the side of looseness while simultaneously defining the big blind's hand: A call (or raise) from this ultra tight player confirms a quality holding. To raise here, then, is to use the power of the bet to win the pot or, at worst, to glean useful information. That's what bets are for! If you chose this path, identify yourself as *sturdy*.

IF YOU RAISED A LOT. Overbetting the pot here might drive out even the loosest player in the small blind, and winning the blinds without a fight is never a bad thing. However, you'll only get a call from the big blind when she has a better hand than yours—which would be the case with your small raise, too. While you'll know where you're at in the hand, you're paying more than you need to for that information. If you choose to make the grandstand raise here, tab yourself as *epic*.

Having answered just one question, then, you now know something about yourself that you didn't know before. You have an assignable label for your play. I want to stress that such labels are not good things or bad things, not right things or wrong things. Though most hold'em players admire the *sturdy* or even the *epic* style of play, there is no absolutely correct action for the situation just described. It may be, for example, that the small blind, while quite loose, is also quite aggressive and can be counted on to bluff away a lot of chips on the flop. If that were the case, you would be correct to play *lax*, and let a flawed player into the pot. Or you could make a case for going *epic* for the specific reason of shutting the loose-but-frisky small blind out of the hand. Likewise, it may be that you've stolen so many blinds recently that you think your foes are irked and ready to play back at you, in which case you'd rather go *wary*, fold, and let them cool off for a while. The point of the exercise, then, is not to get the "right" answer, but to see yourself clearly as you are, a necessary first step toward seeing your opponents as *they* are.

With four possible answers to one question, then, we have identified four types of NLHE player, and assigned them the labels *wary, lax, sturdy,* and *epic*. In fairness, all we're really talking about are *weak-tight, weak-loose, strong-tight,* and *strong-loose,* but frankly I've heard these appellations used so much that they've kind of lost meaning for me, so I opt for more . . . shall we say . . . florid tags. But tags are just tags. Use whatever ones suit you. As I've often noted in these Killer Poker pages, "To name a thing is to own a thing," and the handles you assign, in language you feel comfortable with, will always speak more clearly to you than those that I or anyone else might employ.

Once you've tagged a player, you have tremendous insight into her approach to the game, and can predict other classes of action based on that tag. If you know someone to be a *lax* player, based on the fact that she never seems to attack blinds except with premium hands, what would you expect her to do with middle pairs in middle position? I'd expect her to flat call and hope to flop a set, because that's the sort of neither-here-nor-there move a lax player makes. Turning it around, if you see someone make a first position raise to ten times the size of the big blind, and subsequently show down K-J offsuit, what label would you assign? It wouldn't be *wary,* that's for sure. Even *epic* might not be strong enough. You'd have to go for a whole different label, maybe *suicidal.*

Now I want to edit that last sentence because there's something pejorative about the label *suicidal,* and I'm really trying hard to avoid value judgments here. I mean, can we really say that it's *wrong* to bet ten times the big blind in first position with K-J off? Suppose we knew for sure that we'd get a call from J-T suited? We'd be something on the order of a 2-1 favorite and would want to get as much money as possible into the pot, would we not?

No, yeah, you know what? It *is* wrong to bet ten times the big blind in first position with K-J off, and I can think of five reasons why.

1. I don't know for sure that J-T suited will call.
2. I don't know for sure that A-A isn't out there against me.

3. I won't get action from most worse hands.
4. I risk more chips than the hand warrants.
5. My continuation bet would have to be *huge*.

Can you think of five more? How about just three, since I took all the easy ones?

\>>

So, okay, let's agree that while all playing styles can be situationally correct, some styles are more broadly correct than others. Playing types exist on a spectrum from *too tight* to *too loose,* and generally a playing style that occupies any extreme position—ultra loose, ultra tight, ultra predictable, ultra maniacal, ultra whatever—is less likely to be a successful style because it's less likely to be able to adapt to the real circumstances of a real game against real opponents.

Below is a table of types. Across the top you'll see different sorts of players, and down the left some characteristic preflop betting actions. Take a moment to fill out the table by putting check marks in the boxes where you think given types of players are capable of given moves. For example, someone identified as a calling station is likely to limp with J-T suited, while someone identified as a rock is unlikely to raise in early position with 7-8. Check as many boxes as appropriate; just because a tricky player will naked bluff from the small blind doesn't mean that a tilty player won't, too. Also notice that I've left a couple of spaces blank, both across the top and down the side. Insert a couple of types of your own invention, and then come up with a couple of preflop actions that you can correlate to your types.

A TABLE OF TYPES										
AND THE PREFLOP ACTIONS THEY TAKE										
	ROCK	CALLING STATION		STABLE	TRICKY	BULLY	TILTY		NEWBIE	MANIAC
Open any unraised pot										
Fold to a raise with pocket tens										
Slow play aces										
Limp with J-T suited										
Raise all in on the button with K-K										
Reraise in big blind with Q-Q										
Bluff raise in the small blind										
Raise in early position with 7-8										

For what it's worth, here's how I'd fill out the chart. Don't worry if our assessments don't agree, for your conception of these players is bound to be different from mine, based on your own experience of poker and of the sorts of players you routinely face.

A TABLE OF TYPES
AND THE PREFLOP ACTIONS THEY TAKE

	ROCK	CALLING STATION	COWBOY	STABLE	TRICKY	BULLY	TILTY	KILLER POKER	NEWBIE	MANIAC
Open any unraised pot			✓		✓	✓	✓	✓		✓
Fold to a raise with pocket tens	✓			✓	✓		✓			
Slow play aces	✓				✓				✓	
Limp with J-T suited		✓			✓				✓	
Raise all in on the button with K-K			✓	✓	✓	✓	✓	✓	✓	✓
Reraise in big blind with Q-Q			✓	✓	✓	✓	✓	✓		✓
Bluff raise in the small blind			✓		✓	✓	✓	✓		✓
Raise in early position with 7-8			✓		✓	✓	✓			✓
Flat call in early position with J-J	✓	✓		✓	✓		✓		✓	
Raise in middle position with 7-7			✓		✓	✓	✓	✓		✓

Note how quickly a snapshot emerges of different types of players. With such a snapshot you can start to categorize players with a fair degree of confidence. For instance, if you're up against someone who has raised every unopened pot for the last lap and a half, you know for sure that he's not a rock because rocks tend to call more than raise, even with their good hands. You can also be sure he's not a newbie, because newbies proceed with caution. From such minimal clues and cues, you can then start to make predictions about how these players will perform in other areas. If you've determined someone to be tricky, based on his preflop play, you can take his postflop bets with a grain of salt because a tricky player, by definition, is capable of betting with anything or nothing on the flop.

(Note, by the way, what an advantage a tricky player really has: He's capable of doing anything at any time—is this not a player to be feared?)

Let's test-drive this system and see how it performs.

The game is $300–$500 buy NLHE, meaning that players can buy in for anywhere from $300 to $500. It's a new game, and everyone who sat down, including you, bought in for the maximum. The blinds are $5 and $5. Observing the other players for a while, you are able to assign them the following tentative tags.

TAG TABLE	
SEAT	TAG
1	Tricky
2	?
3	Tighty
4	You
5	Wary
6	Newbie
7	?
8	Juicy
9	?

You have made these assessments based on the players' preflop and postflop betting patterns, and upon a correlation between betting patterns and the hands they ultimately show down. You know not to overvalue such information; that is, you understand your findings to be tentative (which is why there are still a few question marks in your tag table). But you feel you've seen enough actions from certain players to have them—at least provisionally—dialed in.

Seat one has raised under the gun with junk, and also slowplayed a set, and also reraised on a draw, and also bet the river on a naked bluff. It seems reasonable to call this player *Tricky*.

Seat three has only played one hand. That was pocket aces, and though the board was never scary, he check-called the whole way down. It seems reasonable to call this player *Tighty*.

Seat eight has called raises on several hands and subsequently turned over such hands as J-8 suited and ace-little. In fact, she's won the biggest pot so far by getting deep into a raised pot with K♣-9♣, and catching runner-runner clubs to make a flush. This is just one of many manifestly bad plays, so it seems reasonable to call this player *Juicy*.

Armed with these tentative assessments, you now find yourself holding T-T in the big blind. Juicy calls in middle position and Tricky raises from the cutoff seat. Everyone else gets out of the way. What's your pleasure? How would you like to proceed?

Such sketchy information, of course, doesn't give us 100 percent confidence as we go forth, but based on what I see here, I would make a big raise. I believe I can count on Juicy having called with a substandard hand *and* on Tricky having raised with one. Sure, there's a shot that either or both has a real hand here, but neither of these players is Tighty, from whom a call or a raise would be much more likely to indicate real strength.

And if such information is sketchy now, it grows much less sketchy and much more complete as the game goes along.

Here's a little homework for you, if you're game. Photocopy the following blank tag table and take it with you next time you go play. Fill it out as you go along. (Maybe take a couple of extra copies in case you change tables or in case so many players come and go that, like a manager's lineup card in an extra inning ballgame, your table becomes too crossed out and overwritten to be useful.) Don't be afraid to make snap judgments, and don't be afraid to be wrong.

TAG TABLE	
SEAT	TAG
1	
2	
3	
4	
5	
6	
7	
8	
9	

Also don't be at all afraid to get caught using this little analytical cheat sheet, for your foes will predictably respond in one of two ways. Either they'll treat you with respect for taking the game so seriously or else they'll think you're a bit of a fool for thinking you can pigeonhole their play in this way. But here's the thing: No matter how they respond, *their own play will change*. It's our old friend Heisenberg chipping in, reminding us that it's impossible to observe a thing without affecting it. Simply note how people react to the fact of your active observation and include this information in your assessment.

Really, it's a marvelous thing. If you're keeping book on a certain foe and she knows it, she may respond by playing against type—by trying to be, that is, something other than the sort of player she thinks you think she is. Can you see how this will actually put her off her game? Instead of playing her best poker according to her best understanding, she'll waste psychic energy trying to confound your mental picture of her. What she doesn't understand—what they never understand— is that you're constantly updating your assessments based on new available information. When they start making uncharacteristic moves just to throw off your assessment, they actually give you more information to work with. Among other things, they reveal themselves as players capable of making uncharacteristic moves and/or players aware of how others perceive them. Weirdly, then, the more they try to distort your picture of them, the clearer the picture becomes.

Some players will sensibly ignore you completely. They operate on the assumption that you're doing your best to figure them out, by whatever means possible, just as they're doing their best to solve the puzzle that is you. It's worth noting these foes, too, and characterizing them as not so weak-minded as to rise to your feeble bait—or, alternatively, as *so* weak-minded that they don't even see the bait being dangled.

Even if your tag table has no effect on anyone else at your table, it will have a couple of positive effects on you. First, it will give you a clear and immediate snapshot of the people you're playing against. Second, it will keep your head in the game. It might even help your discipline, since you'll be more willing to fold crap hands if you have something to do with your time and attention between deals. This quest for data can become quite a compelling pursuit—so compelling that it trumps the need for action that motivates so many of us to play too many hands.

If the notion of tag tables strikes you as quaint or trivial, that's fine. It is a bit quaint, and it can be quite trivial. But I put it to you that if you're playing proper poker (and I assume you are) you're already keeping tag tables—albeit mental ones—on all your foes as it is. All I'm proposing is to take that which is vague and general and make it more targeted and specific, through the simple expedient of writing things down. You may not need such an expedient, and that's fine, too. It's not unusual, after all, for good players to be able to take a mental survey of the table and appraise all of their opponents to a reasonable degree of accuracy. *Strong . . . weak . . . tilty . . . clueless . . . scary . . . scared . . . kosher . . . angry . . .* these are the sorts of tags we routinely apply to our foes, whether we know it or not. And it is upon the strength of these tags that we make our most critical decisions.

Seat three just raised under the gun. I've got her tagged as straightforward, so I'll take her raise at face value, and fold this here K-J. Had the raise come from seat six, whom I've tagged as chaotic, I'd probably fold also, but for a very different reason. In the former case, I have no trouble putting my opponent on a quality hand; in the latter case, I have a great deal of trouble putting my opponent on any hand, and would rather not mix it up until I'm surer of my own strength.

Such thinking is, I'm sure, not unknown to you. It's the automatic process we all go through in analyzing our opponents. And if you can do an adequate job of collecting, sorting, and storing such information without benefit of cheats such as the tag table, by all means keep doing what you're doing well.

But you know what? There's an even simpler way to parse our foes. Like ice cream in the school cafeteria, it turns out they really only come in two flavors . . .

3

RISK AVERSE AND
RISK AFFINED

So I'm driving to the Commerce Casino with a buddy. Stuck in bad traffic (if you can imagine such a thing in Los Angeles), we fall into a discussion about two broad classes of no limit hold 'em (NLHE) players: those who go looking for a fight at the poker table, and those who shy away. We know tons of players who avoid big confrontations for big money, and quickly assign such players the handle *risk averse*. We also know plenty of players who never met a coin flip they didn't like, or a bluff they wouldn't run, but we stumble in search of an appropriate label for them. My pal suggests *risk inclined* as the opposite of *risk averse,* but I don't think that goes far enough. An inclination is a preference, a tendency, but these players have more than a preference. They have a passion, an avidity. Their nostrils flare as they push their stacks of chips into the pot. Poker for them is all about endorphin shock, and if they can't get that buzz, they don't want to play. In service of capturing the passion of these fastball hurlers, I coin the descriptive phrase *risk affined.* In fact, *affined* actually means *connected* and not, as I would have it, *wild about*; so my buddy chides me, and not for the first time, for warping the language to suit my deviant whim. I quote Lewis Carroll at his raggedy ass: "When I use a word," Humpty

Dumpty said, in a rather scornful tone, "it means just what I choose it to mean—neither more nor less."

Thus do we pass the time in traffic.

Whatever label you assign to such players—and you are of course invited to invent your own—the most important question to ask is, *Which type of player are you?* Take a moment to answer off the top of your head. You'll shortly have an opportunity to explore the question in depth.

>>

I see myself as fairly risk averse, which may surprise you, given the whole *show no mercy, take no prisoners* stance of Killer Poker. I could make some noise about "do as I say, not as I do," but I think it's more correct to say that while I favor a forceful approach to poker, nowhere do I advocate senseless aggression simply for the sake of aggression. Nor am I wired into endorphin shock as so many risk affined players are. Anyway, risk aversion isn't about being timid, it's about eschewing wild gambles, even when we have (or think we have) a marginal edge. It's about waiting for more reliably profitable opportunities downstream. Sure, there are times when we find ourselves running over a table, just betting every hand, but that's not a case of suddenly turning risk affined. Rather, it's usually that the table is so ripe for the taking that attacking it is not a high risk proposition at all. But the truth of big bet poker is that whole stacks can potentially be won or lost on every hand. If you eagerly dive into such situations, you're risk affined. If your involvement is more circumspect, you're risk averse. Simple as that.

Most players start out risk averse in their NLHE careers. This is a natural function of simply not knowing appropriate strategy and tactics for advanced poker play. Absent this crucial information, one relies on simple approaches to the game, the simplest being *get the goods, then bet the goods.* If you think back to your first successful poker experiences, I'll bet you were playing some variation of this approach. You were super tight, stayed away from tricky or marginal situations, and hoped to get your big hands paid off. If you played against foes of equally limited experience but slightly less discipline, you probably found that you could make money off the looseness of others. It's possible, of course, that your own looseness punished your profit, for the Siren's song of poker is about *playing hands,* not *not playing hands,* and though we set out to play tight, our own atavistic urges often get the best of us.

It's this root desire to play more hands that leads players down the path of risk affinity. We note that loose calling is a disaster, but that loose raising has some strategic merit. In the past I have codified that discovery thus:

LOOSE CALL BAD.
LOOSE RAISE GOOD.

Enthusiasm for the loose raise is the hallmark of a risk affined player, and we have all witnessed the effect such a player can have on a game. Watching these one-person wrecking crews in action, we anecdotally reach the conclusion that power poker is the way to go; that where a risk averse player may make a tidy profit, it takes a risk affined player to take over the game. Does this mean that high risk poker is the way to go? Not necessarily, and especially not in NLHE, where blundering into just one trap situation can be a stack killing catastrophe.

It all depends on how you like your variance. Some players would rather play one hand out of twenty, pick up a few blinds, and move on. Others don't mind seeing their stacks fall and rise, confident that the pressure they put on others with their bets will eventually redound to their benefit. You know what? They might both be right. I would expect to see both styles of play trend positive—if played correctly. The problem with risk averse players is that they incorrectly pass on rich opportunities; the problem with risk affined players is that they incorrectly get involved with substandard hands. So, both styles of play can be profitable and both can be unprofitable. News flash, right?

Sun rises in east, film at eleven.

But here's the thing: Players generally tune their risk relationship to emotional, rather than strategic, considerations. They play the way they play because they're comfortable doing so. I'm reminded of the moment in Alex Cox's indie classic *Repo Man,* when Harry Dean Stanton's character, Bud, educates Emilio Estevez's Otto about the repo way of life. "An ordinary person," says Bud, "spends his life avoiding tense situations. A repo man spends his life getting into tense situations." Same with poker. Risk averse players avoid tense situations. Risk affined players eagerly embrace them. You can see, I'm sure, how useful it is to know your foes' proclivities in this regard. Are they glass-half-full optimists who think, *I'm probably ahead; I'd better raise,* or glass-half-empty pessimists who think, *I'm probably beat; I'd better fold?*

Those who calculate such things consider risk averse players to be making a mistake every time they fail to bet with the best of it. In a sense they're right, for if you look off 100 opportunities to bet $100 with a 55 percent to 45 percent edge, you're turning your back on an average net profit of $1,000. But if a player is risk averse and knows it—or knows or fears that he can be outplayed by other, more aggressive, players—then he knows he's only betting himself into trouble by getting involved against players who can make him lay down winning hands to big bets. He'd rather wait for better opportunities. His gut tells him to.

Those who calculate such things consider risk affined players to be making a mistake every time they bet with the worst of it. In a sense they're right, because you can only go to the cookie jar so many times before you get caught. But if a risk affined player knows that a few well placed raises can give her total control over the table, including the right to steal uncontested pots and the chance of getting paid off big-time when she hits a hand, well, she's going to dive right in. She figures her best opportunity is *right now!* Her gut tells her so.

So again we return to the question: What kind of player are you? Do you look for a reason to get involved in a pot? Then you're risk affined. Do you look for a reason to bail? Then you're risk averse. For a more thorough evaluation of your relationship to risk, consider how you'd proceed in the following situations. It's a given that you don't have all the givens here; however, the point of the exercise is not to find the correct action so much as it is to gauge your gut response to risk.

POCKET JACKS FACING A RAISE

You hold pocket jacks in late position. A player in middle position raises it to three times the size of the big blind. Would you call, fold, or raise?

>>

Rare is the player who folds here. There are exceptions, including certain tournament situations, and instances where you have a very strong read on the raiser. In the main, though, the difference between risk averse and risk affined comes down to calling (risk averse) or raising (risk affined). Risk averse players just call because they suspect that their foe has opened with a good ace (the likeliest raising hand) and they want to see a low card flop before they get heavily involved. Risk affined players may suspect that the opener holds a good ace, but get involved anyhow, figuring that their reraise will either win the pot right there or, at minimum, seize post flop initiative and control.

The risk averse player creates a special catch-22 for himself by just calling here, for if the flop comes rich in high cards, he'll probably fold to a bet; however, if the flop comes low and he bets, he won't get much action. Risk averse as he is, he may be content to win a small pot, but he's asking for real trouble in those rare instances when the preflop raiser is in there with a bigger pocket pair. The risk affined player could also run into a big pocket pair, and it could cost him even more, though his preflop reraise at least has the benefit of defining his opponent's hand.

A SUIT, BUT NOT MINE

You hold J♣-T♣ in an unraised big blind. The flop comes T♥-9♥-8♥ and there are three players yet to act behind you. What do you do?

>>

This instance clearly shows how players' risk orientations really color their view of the hand. A risk averse player looks at this flop and thinks, *Well, I only have top pair, weak kicker, and a draw to a straight that may already be beaten and is certainly vulnerable to a flush. Obvious check.* A risk affined player looks at the same flop and thinks, *I have top pair and the right of first action. A bet here will send these turkeys running for cover, and if they don't fold on the flop, I'll bet again on the turn and drive them off then. Obvious bet!*

In the last example, we saw how a risk averse player's flat call left him vulnerable post flop. In this situation, it's the risk affined player whose action creates vulnerability. Unless he's prepared to make a huge flop bet and get everyone all in or all out, he leaves himself open to trouble on subsequent streets. Suppose he makes a pot size bet and gets two callers. The only cards he can love on the turn are a ten or an offsuit seven, and even at that he might be dead already. If the turn is a brick, he can bet again—but again, what if he's betting into a made hand? There are all sorts of hands that beat J-T here. But the risk affined player isn't thinking about that. He's just thinking about blowing away the field with his bets. You can see how even a modestly sophisticated player can lay an effective trap against this player.

TOP PAIR FACING A RERAISE

Holding A-Q, you get a pretty good flop of A-9-7 rainbow. You bet, expecting to win the pot right here, but your foe surprises you with a substantial reraise. How do you go forth?

>>

Risk averse or risk affined, a sensible player will take a moment here to assess the possible range of hands her foe might be on. But that assessment will often be skewed by a player's relationship to risk. A risk affined player will weight her evaluation in favor of weaker enemy holdings, while a risk averse player will weight in favor of the stronger ones. It's a variation on the optimist/pessimist theme, with the risk affined player putting her foe on hands she can beat, like A-J, A-T, or even second pair or a naked bluff. The risk averse player, on the other hand, takes her opponent's raise at face value, and takes it as a sign of a dominating hand such as A-K, two pair, or a set. The risk averse player, in other words, sees danger that might not be there, while the risk affined player overlooks danger that may be real.

This example underscores the importance of knowing yourself and your level of risk affinity. While you'd like to see this situation exactly as it is, no one's perception is that perfect. It's vital that we recognize how our view of a given situation may be tempered by our overall view of the game of poker we play, so that we can adjust for our perception's built-in bias. It's also worth noting that our perception may be affected by contemporaneous outcomes. It's not at all uncommon, for example, for players who are running bad and feeling snakebit to imagine that their foes always have the hand when they bet. Such players fold too frequently because they just can't stand the thought of perpetuating their losing streaks. They are, you might say, situationally risk averse. In extreme cases, they become so risk averse that they simply can't play the game correctly at all.

Interestingly, this same feeling of being snakebit can trigger a response at the other extreme. Having lost and lost and lost, and being now determined to get well quick, a player may consciously or unconsciously deny the obvious evidence that her foes are betting with better hands. She bets every hand as if it were the nuts and ends up bashing herself against the rocks of her own tilt.

BIG RIVER BET (OR BLUFF?)

You hold top pair/top kicker in late position against a single player who is capable both of chasing draws and driving bluffs. The river puts a third flush card on board and your foe bets all in. Will you look her up or lay it down?

>>

In the "it depends" world of poker, it's impossible to know, based on this sketchy information, whether to call here or not. You don't know the pot size, your foe's tendencies and tells, a dozen other things. But that's not really the point. The point is that one's relationship to risk not only colors perception but also influences action. In this instance, the risk averse player will fold specifically because he *is* risk averse. Won't give it a second thought. *She was on a draw and she got there, oh well. I'm certainly not going to call $300 (or $3,000 or whatever) just to give her the smug satisfaction of showing the winner. I'll make the good laydown.*

The risk affined player, meanwhile, may do a rough calculation of the percentage chance that his foe is bluffing, and make or not make the call accordingly. Most likely he'll make the call because, being risk affined, he's likely to "calculate" bluffing odds in such a way as to justify the call he really wants to make. A truly risk affined player will rationalize action even when he knows he's beaten. *I'll call to keep you honest* really means *I'll call because I want to, no matter what.*

I don't have to tell you that neither of these approaches is correct because neither does the sensible, emotionally neutral job of weighing the circumstances and making a dispassionate decision based on available information. I also don't have to tell you that not all players are capable of this dispassionate approach.

And here we come to the salient point.

If you do nothing—*nothing!*—more than sort your foes into the categories of risk averse and risk affined, you give yourself a powerful tool for profit. Consider this last example again, and now imagine that you're the one who's first to act when that scary flush card comes. If you know that your foe is risk averse, you'll bet every time, because you know he'll fold more than he should. If you know that your foe is risk affined, you'll only bet when you have the goods because you know he'll call more than he should. Players who betray their feelings about risk, then, are essentially handing you a big cudgel to club them with. Thank them very much.

How do you figure out if your foes are risk averse or risk affined? The truth is, you already know, by the simple litmus test of loose and tight: If they play a lot of pots, they're risk affined; if they don't, they're not. While it's true that a risk averse player might hit a run of cards he has no choice but to play—or a risk affined player a run of cards even *he* must fold—in the main a player's frequency of participation is a rock-solid indicator of risk relationship. Particularly online, where sniffer software like Poker Tracker will calculate calling frequency for you, this information is pathetically easy to gather. But even if you have to use the anecdotal evidence of your own eyes, you can quickly and easily sort your foes into preflop loose and preflop tight. Then extrapolate that information into postflop play. That's the cudgel. That's money in your pocket.

Is it that easy? *Yes,* it's that easy. Even good players—players who know better than to be ruled by their emotion—have styles and strategies they prefer. These styles and strategies are revealed in their preflop calling frequency—and in many other ways as well, as we can see from the chart below.

SITUATION	RISK AVERSE RESPONSE	RISK AFFINED RESPONSE
Flush draw or straight draw	Check-call	Raise
Middle pocket pairs	Preflop limp	Preflop raise
Missed the flop completely	Fold	Naked bluff
A-4 suited, two limpers	Fold	Raise
8-7 suited, first to act preflop	Fold	Open for a raise
Top pair, bad kicker	Check-call or check-fold	Bet or raise
Six limpers but a bad hand	Fold	Call
Junk holding	Fold	Raise

Everyone—even good players—will give you something to work with. The risk averse ones can be bullied. The risk affined ones can be trapped. It's just a matter of paying attention. No, check that; it's a matter of *productively* paying attention, of building and then retaining a coherent picture of every foe you face. Of course, these pictures will change from time to time. A risk averse player on tilt will be suddenly, chaotically, risk affined. A risk affined player on a tight budget or a short stack will play uncharacteristically snug. But everyone eventually defaults to their true nature. No matter what pains they take to disguise it, their true nature—their real feeling about risk—is routinely revealed in the common, recurring choices of NLHE.

Just the size of a bet is a giveaway. A risk averse player will underbet the pot; a risk affined one will overbet. Make sure you know which is which! Suppose the flop comes A-x-x, and you're holding A-Q. The pot contains $100, and your single foe pushes $250 into it. If she's risk averse, you can figure her for A-K. Risk affined? She might have A-J or worse. In order to make a meaningful judgment about a bet, you need meaningful information about who's making it. So always be prepared to get it.

And then have a plan for the hand.

4

THE PLAN FOR THE HAND

♣ ♠ ♢ ♡

Poker is about general preparedness, this we know. If you go into the game generally ready to meet the challenges you face (such as making meaningful assessments of your foes) you'll do better at the game day in and day out. Poker is about specific preparedness, too. Certain situations recur so frequently that knowing how to play them can spell the difference between success and failure on any given day, or even in the long arc of your poker career. In "the microcosm of the macrocosm," the sum of our small choices creates our overall profit or loss in the game.

Poker is also about solving the puzzle that's presented to us, using all available information to form a plan for a hand. Sometimes the puzzle is trivially easy to solve.

Available information: *I hold 7-2 offsuit.*
Plan for the hand: *Fold.*

Mostly, though, the solution to the puzzle lies in a rough congress of available data shot through with assumptions and suppositions. Absent actually seeing our opponents' cards, or traveling through time to read the flop in advance, the best we can hope for is a deduction about where we stand and how we should proceed. This is why we work so hard to watch our foes, study their betting patterns, remember past plays, pick off tells, and so on. The more information we can gather and process, the easier it is to see the right move in the moment. We must beware tainted information, of course, for savvy players are constantly blowing smoke. But the primary source of tainted information is not them, it's us. In the heat of poker combat, we risk filtering data through hope, fear, anger, greed, or other irrelevant and counterproductive emotions. Can you name some emotions or feelings through which you filter data?

>>

Take the case of an ace on board. With an ace on board and lots of bets and raises, we *must know* that our pocket kings are beaten (no matter how heavily our foes may sigh when they bet and raise). Yet with our perception skewed by a certain sense of entitlement, we see those kings as a hand we "deserve" to win with, and end up calling anyhow. We're not ignorant, just caught up in false optimism. Playing poker this way is like trying to solve a crossword puzzle by letting *frostrup* be an eight-letter word for our thirteenth president. (It's Fillmore.) Wishing just won't make it so.

With these three ideas in mind—preparedness, puzzle solving, and clarity—let's look at some common no limit hold'em situations and seek not only to pick a good plan for the hand but also glean some underlying wisdom we can apply to other situations and other aspects of our game. Let's also note how we (and other players) filter information through hope, desire, or fear.

THE BANE OF BAD SUITED ACES

Even though poker players know better, or should know better, we still see the tendency of many to get involved with bad aces. I'd like to divorce you from this habit by walking you through a typical tempting "bad ace" situation and point out the dead end it generally leads to.

Let's say it's early in a rebuy tournament. Blinds are 10 and 20, and you have most of your starting stack of $800. The player to your left has earned your mental tag *Riot Grrrl* by raising or reraising almost every hand. Such wanton aggression is not unusual in the rebuy stage of a tournament, and in this case she has been well rewarded by a lot of folds from the rocks and Timid Timmies downstream. As a consequence, Riot Grrrl is running well and feeling good. Glancing left, you see her loading up on chips, ready to fire off another raise. You've seen her telegraph enough bets to know that this is not a fake tell, and that she really intends to bet. You hold A♥-7♥. What action do you choose to take, and why?

>>

YOU CAN MAKE A CASE FOR RAISING. I hate a bully when the bully isn't me, and by raising here I might hope to steal the initiative, and the raising prerogative, away from Riot Grrrl. Trouble is, this preemptive strike probably won't work. As she has already tipped her intention to bet, it's not likely that she'll turn timorous and fold to our raise. Based on what we've seen so far, she'll at least call, and possibly reraise, leaving us out of position against an aggressive foe for the rest of the hand. While I generally admire even a reckless raise, I can't see this one having the desired result.

YOU CAN MAKE A CASE FOR CALLING. Riot Grrrl has it in her head to run the table, and so far she's having her way. To limp here is to invite her to raise, and hope to hit a hand you can trap her with after the flop. But what kind of hand are you hoping to hit? Trips or a flush, though lovely, are unlikely. You might even settle for a draw to the nut flush, but can you count on getting enough meek callers to give you proper odds? No. Not with Riot Grrrl running the table and everyone else running scared.

YOU CAN MAKE A CASE FOR A LIMP-RERAISE. I kind of like this plan for the hand because it's bold—albeit risky as well. You just limp, invite her to raise, then make a monster reraise and bet her off her hand. This can work *if* she's attentive enough to read your move as a legitimate play with something like K-K or Q-Q, and *if* she's capable of getting away from her hand. Trouble is, she's shown a lot of friskiness and not a lot of caution so far. Worse, since it's still the rebuy period, she might not be afraid to get felted with K-Q, A-J, 8-8, or any of the other semi-hands she's been raising with around here. Even if she's on a real garbage raise like K-9 offsuit, she's only a 3-2 underdog to your A-7 suited. Plus, what if she doesn't raise, but just limps in behind you? You're stuck with a modest hand in bad position in a situation where you probably have to hit to win.

I WOULD FOLD. That A♥-7♥ certainly looks attractive, especially with a fast and loose player on your left and visions of monster flops krumping like sugar plums in your head. But remember, it's very early in the tournament, and every uncontested pot this Riot Grrrl wins only reinforces her false sense of security. Emboldened by success, she'll keep pushing, and become increasingly overconfident. Sooner or later you'll pick up a strong ace or a good pair, and then your limp-trap or limp-reraise strategy will work just fine. Her overly aggressive strategy will have her primed to give up her chips. But the first iteration of a bad ace is not the time to make your move.

HERE'S THE RUB. The real problem with bad aces is how poorly they play against a whole range of hands and in the face of all sorts of flops. You can't love a flop that contains an ace because you'll only get action from another ace, and the weakness of your kicker must necessarily freeze your own betting aggression. Typically, with an ace on flop you'll either win a small pot without a fight or (if you're not careful) lose a big pot to a better ace. If the flop comes aceless, you're still not home free. Remember, you're dealing with a reckless raiser. Suppose the flop comes something like K-J-T. Are these not just the sort of cards such a raiser is likely to hold? If you go to war here your only weapons are an inside straight draw and a lone overcard. Not so good.

WHAT TO WATCH OUT FOR. Suited aces are devilishly sticky. We hold on to them longer than we should, for while we may be aware that flopping a flush is a long shot (118-1 against, at last math), we nevertheless believe fervently that *this could be the time*. The best way to stay rational about suited aces is to ask yourself how you'd feel if your ace weren't suited. Since suitedness only adds about 3 percent of value to any given hand, in most cases a modest suited ace should be played the same way as a modest unsuited ace: folded without regret.

BOTTOM LINE. Does this mean you should fold all bad suited aces all the time? Of course not. If you know you can get a cheap flop with lots of callers, and if you know you'll get paid off if you hit, there's nothing wrong with taking a flier on the flush—recognizing that the strength of this holding lies in its flush potential, not in its acedness. But remember . . .

JUST BECAUSE YOU *CAN* PLAY A HAND DOESN'T MEAN YOU *MUST* PLAY A HAND.

With a good read, or even a fair read, on the other players at your table, you should be able to predict how the betting will go after it gets past you, and whether you'll be able to take the flop in a favorable situation or not. If your conclusion is that things won't go the way you'd like them to, suspend your wishful thinking and fold.

THE LOW FLOP AND THE CONTINUATION CONUNDRUM

In the mob psychology of poker, most players at a typical table look to the preflop raiser to lead the action postflop. This bet, famously called a *continuation bet,* can bring all sorts of grief to a preflop raiser when the flop misses her hand—especially if the flop comes low and ragged. While she's generally expected to bet (because she raised preflop), she's suspected to have missed the flop (because it's junk). Let's peel back the layers of this conundrum and find a plan for the hand when the flop doesn't go our way.

You're playing in a $500 minimum buy in NLHE cash game with $5 and $10 blinds. Your experience of this table so far is that no one is terribly aggressive or terribly out of line; in short, the game seems tame. But you have to figure that these players are at least reasonably skilled and knowledgeable—else they'd be playing lower. You've been throwing in a few raises and winning a few uncontested pots, and perceive your image to be solid/ stolid. No one's expecting any monkey business out of you. Just now you open in middle position for your standard raise of $25. I'm not assigning you a hand here because in this instance it really doesn't matter what you have. The issue isn't what cards you hold, but what cards your opponents *think* you hold.

So. You get one late position caller, and the blinds both fold. The flop comes 5-3-2 rainbow. Action's on you.

>>

WHY THIS FLOP IS A PROBLEM. The situation seems to cry out for a continuation bet, but who would believe that a solid/

stolid player like you would have a piece of *that* flop? A flop containing *wheelhouse* cards (ace through ten) would have been so much nicer for you, since you could represent a fit with the sort of hands a solid/stolid player bets. But that's not the case here, and the first thing we poker players must always do is

ACCEPT WHAT IS.

So there you are, hanging out on a ragged flop, hoping your foe will put you on a pocket pair, but fearing that he'll put you on your likeliest holding, unpaired overcards, instead. If you bet, you run the risk of getting messed with by someone who assumes—probably rightly—that the flop was a complete whiff for you.

HOW IT LOOKS IF YOU BET. Come out betting here and you're basically saying, "Yeah, I'm making a continuation bet, whatcha gonna do about it?" Many foes will fold, God love them, because they're Timmies who have no stomach for a fight. Trouble is, not all foes are Timmies. Many are strong and savvy, and they have lots of options here, including just calling and basically daring you to fire again on the turn. They may have in mind to run a *program* on you, a betting sequence in which they flat call any bet on the flop and raise any bet on the turn (or bet if you check), thus extracting maximum value from your obligatory continuation bets before taking the pot away. Against such foes who don't give up on the flop, you'll usually have to shut it down on the turn, and fold to any bet. That's a pretty meek play, costing lots of image equity, not to mention chips. Yielding control of the hand, then, is a must to avoid. But can you *seem* to yield control while still maintaining it? Let's see . . .

YOU HATE TO CHECK, BUT STILL . . . If betting the flop and checking the turn is meek, then checking the flop is mousier still. The very best you can hope for is an equally passive foe content to check behind you. If that happens, you do pick up some room to move on the turn. For instance, if the turn card is low—another five, say—you can bet as if to say, "Well, since you don't want this pot, I guess I'll take it with my mere ace high." Alternatively, if a wheelhouse card comes, you can bet it like you own it, now projecting, "Yes, I was out of line with my preflop raise, but I got a free card on the flop and got lucky on the turn so now the pot is mine." Of course, there's no guarantee that your foe will check behind you on the flop; he may bet, in which case you'll probably have to pass. Then again, if he should check the flop, he could hit his card on the turn (or decide that your check on the flop means you're definitely lying/stealing now), in which case he'll attack back on the turn and try to take the pot away then. Raising before the flop and checking on the flop, then, represents a greater loss in image equity, though not in chips. However, certain of your trickier foes will hand you an elegant exit from this bind.

IF YOUR FOE IS FRISKY . . . It may be that you can count on a given opponent to try to claim any pot where you show weakness. While at first blush this seems like bully behavior, it's really not so bad for you, for it allows you to assign a higher than usual probability that he's bluffing. In this case, if you make the play I now dignify with the label *continuation check* (ha!) you invite Mr. Frisky to bet. Then you go ahead and raise, signaling that you've either trapped him with a better hand (that premium pair he didn't think you have but can't completely discount) or goaded him into a bluff, which you're now snapping off. Granted, this move takes guts, because you're voluntarily putting money into a pot when you could otherwise get away from the hand for the price of just your preflop raise. But it does yield the benefit of keeping your image strong and confounding. Showing yourself capable of a check-raise where a straightforward continuation bet is called for will earn you some image equity now, and may also give you a free card in a later hand, when another continuation conundrum appears.

WHAT YOU ARE AFRAID OF? When the flop comes low, your main fear is that, even though it's a ragged board, somehow it hit your foe's hand. Well, guess what? Even though her logic tells her that you missed, too, her fear will at least entertain the possibility of your having found a fit. At minimum, she knows that you're capable of raising with a big pocket pair, and if that's what you've got here, you're not really too worried about whatever this ragged flop contains. Remember,

TWO THIRDS OF THE TIME, ANY TWO UNPAIRED CARDS DO *NOT* HIT A PAIR ON THE FLOP.

Remember also that with a low ragged flop any pair your foe makes here must necessarily be a low one. Let's say she called with a bad ace (we know how we feel about those) and now her A-5 has turned into top pair, top kicker. But it's a fragile top/top. She may already be trailing your big pocket pair; even if she's not, any non-ace high card on the turn must necessarily give her pause. In any case, her likeliest holding is not top/top, but rather random overcards. If she has overcards without an ace, she really can't afford to call, even if she suspects that you're a lying sack of cheese stuck on a continuation bet, for though you may be way out of line with a mediocre ace, she still has to hit to win. In other words, *logic* tells her you have nothing, but *evidence* tells her she has nothing, too. In this situation, many players will choose the safe course, and fold when you bet.

SOMETIMES YOU DO WHAT'S EXPECTED. You're expected to make a continuation bet here, and even though you feel like you're exposed and vulnerable, I think you pretty much have to follow through . . . *because your foe feels exposed and vulnerable, too!* Even if he figures you for a naked steal, he needs to have a hand that can beat a steal. He may not have the stomach for a fight, but how can you push him off the hand if you *don't push?* Bet, and give him a chance to fold.

THE PREFLOP RAISE AND THE DELICATE DANCE. In most cases, we want to be the aggressor. In most cases, we want to be the ones putting in the preflop raises. This means that we're going to face the continuation conundrum many, many times in one form or another—literally, every time the flop doesn't hit our hand. For the sake of avoiding predictability, we can't play it the same way every time, but most of the time we're going to try to keep the initiative in the hand. The two controlling ideas here are:

1. IT'S HARD TO MAKE A HAND.
   Just because you missed doesn't mean your foe didn't miss, too.
2. THEY CAN'T FOLD IF YOU DON'T BET.
   And if they do fold, you win not just chips, but image equity, too.

THE UTILITY UNDERBET

Someone gave you a gift. An uncharacteristic limpfest in an otherwise aggressive low buy in an NLHE game has put you in the big blind in a four-way pot with an unraised free look at the flop. Blinds in this game are $1 and $2, and you have about $100 in front of you, as do the other three players. Holding K♣-3♣, you flop the nut flush draw: A♣-T♦-6♣. There's $9 in the pot (including the small blind's surrendered dollar). (And yes I know there are rake considerations, but let's keep our lives simple, shall we?) How would you like to proceed?

>>

FREE CARD, ANYONE? Maybe you'll just check here. If everyone else checks, you'll get to see the turn card for free, and possibly hit your flush then. I can see two problems with this plan. First, with two wheelhouse cards up there, it's likely that one of the limpers has a piece of this flop and will bet. Second, they see those two clubs as clearly as you do, and will be disinclined to give anyone a free draw to the flush here. Oh, third problem: Suppose they do all check and you hit your flush on the turn. How much action are you likely to get then?

HOW ABOUT A BIG SEMI-BLUFF? You could make a pot-size bet, hoping that everyone will fold or, if they call, that you'll connect on the turn. Trouble is, you're out of position. If you bet now and get callers, you'll need either a club on the turn or sufficient stones to fire again at the pot. But suppose you run into a big reraise? You'll be facing a big bet from a player who may or may not be bluffing, with unfavorable odds for your draw. Your big semi-bluff on the flop, then, puts you out ahead of your hand and puts you at the mercy of the cards, or your foes' weakness. Cards may fall, but you can't count on weakness. As we have identified this game as generally aggressive, we have to wonder why they all turned passive on this hand preflop. Either someone is slow playing a big pair or there are a lot of second-rate hands out there, like A-8, K-J, 7-7—none of which you can currently beat. Bottom line: Big semi-bluff equals big semi-trouble.

I LIKE A SMALL BET HERE. There's $9 in play. Suppose you bet $3. If you get no callers, that's fine, you win the pot right here. But I think you will get callers. Bad aces will call, looking to hit their kickers. Worse flush draws than yours will be delighted that you made the "mistake" of giving them correct odds to call. Even something like Q-J might call, taking an incorrect (but cheap) flier on an inside straight. If you get so much as a single caller, you've got a pot that gives you roughly the correct odds to try for your flush on the turn (4 to 1 or better, depending on the number of callers).

WHAT IF YOU GET RAISED? It's not the end of the world. If the raise comes big, you can get away from your hand, having used a teaser bet to flush a big holding out of the weeds. If the raise comes small, though, you simply recalculate the odds and see where you stand. It may be that you've priced yourself into the pot twice on the same betting round. Suppose you start by betting $3. Now there's $12 in the pot. Two callers build the pot to $18. Then someone makes it $10 to go. There's a fold, and it's back to you. The pot contains $28, and you have to call $7. There's your 4–1 odds again, and it's highly likely that both of the $3 callers will chip in another $7 as well, giving you an even better price for your call.

IF YOU MISS ON THE TURN, UNDERBET AGAIN. Suppose you made a small bet on the flop and just got called. Now the turn comes 2♦—a true hold'em brick. Go ahead and underbet again. You can give yourself the same favorable odds in exactly the same way. Say the pot is $21 ($9 preflop plus your $3 flop bet and three callers). A small bet here (say, $7) may look like a *hoover* bet from a really strong hand, designed to suck in callers. Or, it may be an enticement to players drawing to worse hands than yours. As soon as one player calls, you've got odds for your flush draw. If you face a raise, you make the same calculation as before, sticking around if the odds warrant and folding if they don't. Of course if a club comes on the turn, you have all sorts of options, including making the very same small bet and hoping that someone raises so you can come over the top.

A NEW WAY OF LOOKING AT IMPLIED ODDS. We often think of implied odds in terms of the action on subsequent streets: "If I call this bet now, will I be able to win enough later?" In this instance, we're looking at the implied odds surrounding a bet you *make* rather than a bet you *call*. When your underbet money goes into the pot, you're not getting the right price, but as soon as someone else's money goes in you *are*. If no one else calls, you don't get the right odds, but you *do* get the pot! Plus, by betting, even underbetting, you keep aggressiveness on your side, never a bad thing. Against the right sort of opponents, you can actually give yourself correct odds to draw over and over. If you hit, you'll win the pot, and if you miss, you get away from the hand at minimal cost. It pays to think ahead.

THE UTILITY UNDERBET. Many people misconstrue the odds of their drawing hands. They know that they're, for example, 2–1 to complete a four-flush with two cards to come, but forget (or conveniently ignore) the fact that they won't necessarily get to see two cards for the price of a call on the flop. Naturally this is wrong, but it's a common mistake, commonly made. The reason for underbetting your draws, then, is to manipulate the size of the pot so that you get the right price to draw every time you put money in the pot. There's a problem, though. This bet is so useful that it quickly becomes transparently so. Once your savvy opponents recognize that you're trying to price yourself into your draws, they'll make you pay with big raises whether they have a hand or not. To preempt this, throw in the odd underbet in other situations as well, especially ones where no straight draw or flush draw is present on board. In this way, you'll disguise the utility of the underbet and you can use it effectively when you need it most.

ONE LAST THING. If you're on the receiving end of a utility underbet, don't be so quick to merely accept the favorable odds you see being offered. Ask yourself *why* that bet's so small. There are three possible reasons.

a. It's a straightforward utility underbet.
b. It's a hoover.
c. Your foe doesn't know any better.

You should be able to deduce the reason for the underbet, based on its bettor of origin. If you suspect B, you should fold, but if you suspect A or C, don't just call—*raise!* With such strategies as the utility underbet, you want to know not just the move, but the countermove, too.

ORPHAN, ORPHAN, WHO'S GOT THE ORPHAN?

There's a class of crap flops you see over and over again, flops like 7-7-2, 9-4-4, 8-4-2. I call these *orphan flops* because they contain the types of cards that sensible, kosher players are unlikely to hold, and thus their pots are homeless waifs just looking to be adopted by the first person to bet. Should that person be you? Let's break it down.

Suppose you've raised in late position with A-K and gotten a call from a mid-position limper. The flop comes 8-4-4 rainbow. Your foe checks to you. Should you bet?

>>

NOT JUST YES, BUT HELL YES! As a rule, any time there's an orphan flop and no one else has tried to adopt it, I'm going to put a bet out there and see if I can take it home. Before I do that, though, I'll ask myself some quick questions.

1. How does my foe like this flop?
2. Does she know I adopt orphans?
3. Will she yield just the same?

ORPHANS DON'T INSPIRE INVOLVEMENT. Does my foe like this flop? If she has 8-8 or 4-4, she loves it. Other pocket pairs, especially large ones, will look good here, but it's 16–1 against her holding any pocket pairs here; and if she had a premium one, I think I'd have heard about it preflop. Nor is she likely to have 8-4 offsuit, not having twice put money in the pot already. Also—and this is the hallmark of a true orphan—there are no straight draws or flush draws to get excited about. Not even so much as a wheelhouse card. The only reasonable, and reasonably common, good hand she can have here that connects to this flop is A-8. Way more often than not, she has nothing. So, no, she probably doesn't like this flop.

BUT I'M A LYING SACK OF CHEESE. Doe she know I adopt orphans? It so happens that I've been playing an FNL (fast 'n' loose) style at this table for a while. I've raised with so many peculiar holdings and bet at so many ragged flops that my foe has no particular reason to believe I've hit a hand here. On the other hand, I've raised with so many peculiar holdings and bet at so many ragged flops that she has no particular reason to believe I've missed, either. She's seen me raise with A-A—but also with 9-8 suited. Where am I now? Thanks to my all-over-the-place play, she doesn't know. So, yes, she knows I adopt orphans, but in this case that information clouds as much as it clarifies. (Obviously if she doesn't know I adopt orphans, it's a straight steal: I bet; she credits me with a piece of the flop; she folds; next case.)

WILL SHE GIVE IT UP? Will she yield? That's the key consideration. Let's say she knows I'm FNL. Does this mean that she'll play back at me? Yes, occasionally . . . but probably only on those occasions when she thinks she's ahead in the hand. Most of the time she can easily convince herself that she's trailing. If she has something like Q-J suited, for instance, she's in a real pickle. She may know beyond doubt's shadow that I'm a brazen waif thief—and still choose not to call. Why? Because even (or especially) brazen waif thieves bet with naked aces. Suppose she calls here and misses (which she's more likely to do than hit, no matter what she holds). She might face another bet on the turn, and once again have to decide where I'm at. Here's where being a lying sack of cheese really comes in handy. Since I could be in there with anything or nothing at all, I either have a hand or I don't, and she has to guess right—not just once, but twice. Most players find it easier to surrender to an unpredictable player than to get involved, even if they have reason to believe that the unpredictable player is bluffing.

WHAT IF THEY CHECK-RAISE? Occasionally, your foes will play back at you. This shouldn't concern you too much. In most cases they're mustering the maximum level of trickiness they're capable of: check-raising with a real hand. Go ahead and fold—but while you're folding ask yourself why they chose to fire back on this particular orphan flop and not the last one or the one before. The answer is not that they finally got fed up with your thieving ways and decided to show you who's boss. Of course they're fed up with your thieving ways. They've been fed up all along. The difference is *this time they have a hand.*

AND WHAT IF THEY JUST CALL? From your foe's point of view, the best defense against your orphan steal is the simple flat call. It doesn't tell the stealer whether the defender has a hand, half a hand, or no hand at all. So if it's called on the flop and checked to you on the turn, probably don't fire again. And don't mind getting caught stealing from time to time. That just reinforces your FNL image. You can even release to a bet on the river, secure in the knowledge that anything but abject surrender on your foe's part probably indicates a real hand. If she's capable of check-calling and then betting out on a bluff, more power to her. Just note that she's able to be that tricky and resolve not to attack orphans so promiscuously against her again. But if you're in the right kind of game, most of your foes are simply not that tricky.

WHEN YOU ADOPT ORPHANS, YOU GIVE YOUR FOE A CHOICE. You give her the option to yield that orphan or try to take it away from you. Sure she wants to catch you stealing, but she wants to catch you *when she has a hand*. That's why it's so easy to attack orphans consistently and to back down when you take heat. There will be another orphan along in a few minutes, and you can go after that one instead. If you decide that your foes have figured out that you'll fold to reraises, then just shut down your adoption agency for a little while, either until you happen to have a hand or until they've forgotten what a lying sack of cheese you are.

THE PLAN FOR THE HAND. Your big decision in adopting an orphan is how far you'll push your effort. Before you bet the flop, you have to ask yourself whether you'll bet again on the turn—fire the second barrel, as Doyle Brunson puts it— or shut down your steal attempt. And if you're still involved at the river, what then? Of course, your subsequent decisions will be based on the turn and river cards, but the decision you make on the flop is based on two things: you, and your opponent. If you have the right image and the right foe, go ahead and steal that orphan, but if these conditions aren't met, there's no harm in not contesting this pot at all.

WARNING: NOT ALL ORPHANS ARE ORPHANS. While a flop like 9♣-9♥-4♦ is not likely to ignite anyone's passion, something such as 9♣-9♥-8♥ is a whole different brand of baby. In the latter case, there are possible straight draws and flush draws, and these draws create opportunities for your clumsy foes and deft foes alike. The clumsy ones will take whatever draws they happen to have, whether they have odds or not. The deft ones—grr, we hate this type—will call you on the flop, and bet any scare card on the turn. If that happens, you'll probably have to get away from the hand, and that's a shame. So pick your orphans with care. If it's a pure orphan, go after it. But if it offers possibilities for either a legitimate call or a legitimate bluff, don't treat it like an orphan, 'cause it's not. Also remember that orphan plays, like all naked bluffs, work better against few opponents. If a crowd sees the flop, the chances that it's a pure orphan are greatly diminished, as are the chances of avoiding a nasty custody fight.

ORPHANS: THE SUBSET. Orphans are a definable subset of all the flops you'll see. You can play them or not as you see fit, but I think there's a broader benefit in getting involved with them: You show your foes that you're willing to mix it up, to take stabs at flops that may or may not hit your hand. This destabilizes them and makes them see you as dangerous and tricky. The dollar cost of going after orphans is often low, but the image dividend can be high.

BIG SCARY ORPHANS

Your basic orphan flop is so barren of possibilities that most people will let you have it without a fight. Another type of orphan flop, *the big scary orphan,* is so rich in possibilities that your foes might let you have that one, too. Big scary orphans are flops like A-A-K, K-Q-Q, or K-Q-J suited. Let's see about adopting them.

Suppose you've been card dead for a while, just sittin' on your hands an' waitin' for better times. It's folded around to you in late position, and your image is sufficiently tight that you can open with, well, anything, and still look like a kosher player making a kosher raise. Only the big blind calls, a Wally who'll see a flop with anything from Q-J to a bad ace to a small pocket pair. The flop comes K♥-K♠-A♠ and it's checked to you. What will you do?

>>

Wow, that is one scary flop!
So go ahead and bet into it.
After all, you raised preflop, right?
And your image is currently snug.
While your foe should consider it unlikely that you have A-A or K-K, due to those hands' sheer rarity, he can easily put you on a good ace or a good king, since these are the sort of hands a (presently perceived as) tight player like you likes to raise with. Note that you couldn't adopt a low orphan here because your image is not sufficiently loose for you to be assumed to have the requisite "anything or nothing at all."

WORK YOUR IMAGE. Your plan for this hand is to find a fit among your image, the bets you've made, and the possibilities the board presents. In this case, your image says that you're betting a big hand. The combination of your perceived big hand and a big flop will drive most foes' cards to the muck. Why? Because they don't want to be catastrophically wrong. Someone holding T-T here, for instance, can easily make a "good laydown" rather than chase what he assumes to be a two-outer.

YOU'RE LESS AFRAID OF A BAD ACE THAN A BAD KING. While loose players will defend their blinds with both sorts of hands, it's the bad king that will cause you real trouble here, as it presents a natural, practically risk-free, trapping opportunity for your friend in the big blind. Of course a bad ace is no picnic for you, either, for your foe may figure that any high card on the turn or the river will give him at least a chopped pot. In all events, if your foe calls too eagerly on the flop, go ahead and shut it down on the turn. Again, it's better to get caught stealing—you can always revise your play to fit your new image—than to bluff off a lot of chips. On the other hand, here's a case where the bold player can fire that second barrel on the turn. Remember that you're perceived as tight. If the turn comes a brick and you bet again, you're just confirming what your foe fears: that a legitimate hand hit a legitimate flop and he's drawing dead or nearly so.

DO YOU EVEN WANT TO PLAY THIS HAND? Viewed through a certain filter, attacking this big scary orphan could be seen as a reckless adventure. You have nothing. Your foe could have a huge hand. And here you are, blithely betting into him. Why not just check behind him and see what the turn and the river may bring? You know what? You can go that route. It's certainly safe enough, and there's nothing wrong with playing it safe in a high volatility game like no limit Texas hold'em. But if you consistently play it safe, you predictably become—here's the bad news—a consistent, predictable player. In the next chapter we'll take a look at how to unravel consistency and predictability, but first I'd like you to try something.

In this chapter we've set up some situations and examined various plans for various hands. This, of course, only scratches the surface of available hands to examine, so won't you please spend a few minutes inventing situations, examining possible approaches, and settling on a plan for the hand? I'll start you off, and you can carry on from there. (By the way, if inventiveness fails you, just borrow from situations you've seen or hands you've played. The point of the exercise is to get good at analyzing table events away from the table.)

- In a $3–$5 blind, $200 buy in game, an early position player, risk affined, opens for $15. You call in middle position with 9-9, and the risk affined button also calls. Money is equally deep, about $200. The flop comes 7-8-T. The original bettor bets $35. What's your plan for the hand?
- It's a limpfest! Eight callers see a $2 blind in a $1–$2, $100 buy in game. You have Q-Q in the big blind, and it's your option to check or raise. There are too many players to identify individually, but with all those limpers, you can figure the table to be generally weak and loose. What's your plan for the hand?
- You hold 9-J in an unraised big blind against two kosher limpers. The flop comes A-K-3. What's your plan for the hand?

Note that in this last example there's a paucity of real information. That's okay. Fill in the blanks as you see fit. The assumptions you make in building thought-problems like this are not all that different from the assumptions you make in real game situations. So build a couple more, and then we'll move on.

-
-
-

5

INCONSISTENT AND
UNPREDICTABLE

♧ ♤ ◇ ♡

In a perfect poker world (from our point of view) all of our foes would play consistently and predictably. They'd raise when they have strong hands, muck when they have weak ones, and behave in all ways according to clear patterns. In no limit hold'em especially this would be a tremendous boon, since we'd never get trapped and always know exactly where we stood in big bet situations. Given that we'd like all our foes to be consistent and predictable, doesn't it follow that they'd like the same from us? And does it not then follow that for us to thwart them, we must, in fact, be inconsistent and unpredictable?

Maybe it follows and maybe it doesn't. I know many successful NLHE players who never stray from their chosen approach to the game. They are consistently selective, for example, only getting involved with premium hands, and gleaning their profit from opponents too loose and too unobservant to notice that when they bet they always have the goods. Against tighter, more observant foes, of course, these Constant Johnnies have trouble making money because they have trouble getting action on their hands.

Nor is pure rampant inconsistency a recipe for success. We've all encountered aggressive players who don't need much of a hand, or even any hand, to throw in a raise or two or six. It doesn't take us long to recognize this disconnect between bet size and hand strength, and to counter it by discounting the value of their raising requirements and adjusting our calling and reraising strategies accordingly. Weirdly, then, players can become predictable in their unpredictability and suffer accordingly.

So if pure consistency is a flawed strategy, and pure inconsistency is likewise flawed, where does that leave us? Can we find a middle ground? Can we find a state of consistent inconsistency, a more sophisticated iteration of the novice player's mantra, *they can't figure out your strategy if you don't have one?* We can certainly try, but there's a readily apparent problem with this. In order to play inconsistently, mustn't we sometimes stray from the path of perfect poker, or in other words just *play wrong?* We need only revisit David Sklansky's Fundamental Theorem of Poker to see what a bad idea *that* is.

> *Every time you play a hand differently from the way you would have played it if you could see all your opponents' cards, they gain; and every time you play your hand the same way you would have played it if you could see all their cards, they lose. Conversely, every time opponents play their hands differently from the way they would have if they could see all your cards, you gain; and every time they play their hands the same way they would have played if they could see all your cards, you lose.*[1]

In truth I understand Sklansky no better than Sanskrit, but I think he's driving at something like this: If you have pocket kings preflop and you know your foe has pocket aces, every time you call his bet you're wrong, because you know your holding is a loser to his. Turning it around, if you have pocket aces preflop and you know your foe has pocket kings, every time you fail to raise, you're making the mistake of not ex-

---

1. David Sklansky, *The Theory of Poker* (Las Vegas: Two Plus Two Publishing, 1994), 16.

tracting maximum value from your hand. But wait a sec. What if you know not just your opponent's cards but also his predilections? What if you knew that he'd fold to your raise preflop, but move all in on any ragged flop if you just call? Would you not then be better off—I mean, *much* better off— just calling with your aces and taking him off his whole stack?

In the world of real players, you don't expect pocket kings to fold to a raise, so therefore you probably should raise, just like Sklansky says. But let's stretch this hypothetical consistency to the snapping point. Let's say you're so consistently tight that the only hand you ever raise with is pocket aces. Your very consistency, then, would give your foe enough information to "know" you have pocket aces and, according to Sklansky, correctly fold. Again, in the world of real players, none of us is that consistently tight; nor are most of our foes that keen in their reads. It's the keen read, in fact, that leads to the good laydown, or to any other circumstance in which you draw the correct conclusion even though your information is incomplete. Since information is always incomplete, the job of all poker players is to make the best possible decision based on the best available information. And *this* is why we must be inconsistent and unpredictable: to degrade the quality of information we provide to our foes. In other words, while part of playing correctly is consistently betting with the best of it,

PART OF PLAYING CORRECTLY
IS BEING HARD TO FIGURE OUT.

Think about it. Think about all the times you've been up against a player who simply confounds you. You never seem to know where he's at in the hand and the attendant emotion you feel is *frustration*. That's quite a one-two punch: confusion plus frustration. It's hard to play effective poker in such a state of mind, and it's hard to play effectively against those who put us in this place. They get us leaning the wrong way; we fold when they're bluffing, call when we're beat, and just basically hate life. Against such foes we frequently opt out, choosing not to mess with them rather than chance being wrong or—as is always a threat in NLHE—catastrophically wrong.

Knowing how vexing such foes can be, then, we should certainly seek to *be* such a vexing foe to our foes. But we're still stuck, right? Between making the correct play and correctly mixing up our play? Not necessarily. I can think of many situations in NLHE where there's more than one correct way to play. Here are three that come quickly to mind.

I hold K♥-Q♥ on the button and it's folded around to me. I figure to have a better hand than the random hands held by the blinds—but I also figure to be able to outplay both of these weaker players after the flop if I let them into the pot. Therefore, flat calling, raising small, or raising big might all be correct.

I hold a small pocket pair in early position. I think, but am not sure, that if I flat call I'll start a limpfest that will give me correct odds to try for a set. I also think, but am not sure, that I might run into big raises. So I can make a case for either calling or folding, and would feel that either choice is right.

First to act after the flop, I've picked up a flush draw against two opponents. If I check, they might bet, giving me a chance to put in a big check-raise semi-bluff and blow them off the pot. Alternatively, I might check-call a small bet and ride pot odds to the turn. Or, I could bet out and try to win the pot right now. Then again, if I check, and there's a bet and a big reraise, I might have to fold. As far as I can tell, I can make a credible argument for betting out, check-calling, check-raising, and check-folding.

Can you think of—or recall from your experience—similar situations where credible arguments can be made for different courses of action?

>>

This is really a key consideration of NLHE. Unlike its limit cousin, where the fixed betting structure and odds of the game separate so many plays into clearly right and clearly wrong, NLHE is a much more fluid, much more dynamic game. Consider the amount of your preflop raise in, say, a $200 buy in NLHE game with $3 and $5 blinds. In some games, a raise to $10 will fold the field; in others, a raise to $40 seems just to draw them in. You couldn't say that the size of either raise was correct without appropriately fitting it into the particular circumstance.

IN NO LIMIT HOLD'EM,
THE OCEAN IS BLUE BUT IT'S ALSO WET.

This is a seductive thought, but let's be clear that what we're looking for are situations or plays where we can be unpredictable and inconsistent but still *generally* correct. Absent that clarity, we might fall into the familiar trap of glorifying unprofitable looseness with the label "variation." I think the thinking would go something like this.

Okay, I'm in late position holding 9-6 suited. There's been a bet and a raise in front of me. Normally I'd never play a crap hand like this, but I'm afraid that my opponents perceive me as consistently tight. If I call here—in the name of inconsistency and unpredictability—they'll never put me on the hand I have, and if I happen to hit and win, they'll never be able to put me on a hand ever again!

Granted, there's an unpredictability benefit to be realized if you should happen to hit your (substandard) hand. But this thinking is flawed—*way* flawed—because in most cases your unpredictability will never be exposed and therefore exploited. Since you really have to hit the flop twice with this hand— two paired cards or two cards to an open-ended straight or a flush—you'll miss almost all the time. The likeliest outcome for this call, then, or for any of its class (e.g., K-2 suited, J-T offsuit) is a meek fold on the flop. Calling with a bad hand is not deception, variation, unpredictability, trickiness, or inconsistency. It's just a bad, loose call and a tragic waste of chips. Of course, if you're making an RWC (*raise with cheese*) for the sake of selling a maniac image, that's a whole different thing. Always ask yourself if your inconsistency has a purpose (other than pure self-indulgence) and always put your inconsistency in the context of your larger goal: taking over the table; and confusing and confounding your foes to the point where they cede control of the game.

Still and all, I really feel like this discussion needs a disclaimer:

> WARNING!
>
> Poor play in the name of unpredictability can be hazardous to your stack!

While I believe that a flexible approach to NLHE is a successful approach, and while I further believe that it's profitable to play an array of hands beyond the so-called premium ones, don't take any of this discussion as a license to come off your game and play a lot of crap hands. Don't let "variation" take you into the realm of calling with the worst of it. Don't let the Siren's song of unpredictability trick you into firing futile bluffs into foes with made hands. That way lies madness.

Or anyway poverty.

In the name of mixing up your play, look for situations where your hand can go in divergent, but still generally correct, directions. Most folding situations are folding situations, no matter what. Likewise, in certain situations it's so overwhelmingly correct to raise (to protect a big hand against a big draw, for instance) that variation is not called for. Between these extremes, though, there are a number of common NLHE occurrences in which different paths are possible. Let's take a look at some now.

PACKAGE HANDS

A package hand is a sub-premium hand that you add into your "package" of raising hands for the sake of deception. Middle suited connectors and middle pocket pairs are typical package hands. If your play in the game has endowed you with a tight image, either because you've been playing tight or because you've been getting poor cards, raising with your designated package hands is a good way to—gently—expand your universe of playing hands while at the same time distorting your foes' vision of you as a get-the-goods, bet-the-goods type.

Let's say you're in late position with 9♣-8♣ and three or four players have limped into the pot before you. Let's further say that cards and circumstance have conspired to keep you sidelined in the game so far, such that you haven't played a hand for a raise since you sat down. In this instance you could consider calling, since the limpfest is on and a hand like 9-8 suited likes lots of callers and no raisers, looking to flop a draw. You could also make a case for folding, since 9-8 suited is certainly nothing to write home about and you're a favorite not to hit your hand anyhow. Alternatively, you could claim 9-8 suited as one of your package hands and fire off a variation raise, since most foes will respect the first raise from a heretofore inactive player—especially if you raise into traffic, as is the case here.

There are a couple of things to think about. First, don't raise unless you're prepared to make a big bet here, and probably bet again on the flop. It's fine if you have no stomach for such risky business. You'll find other, better, opportunities to raise later. But if you do make this package raise you're representing a big hand, and if you can't, or won't, sell it strongly enough then you're better off not putting it on the market in the first place.

Also, recognize that your image must be right. The purpose of being inconsistent and unpredictable is to cut against the grain of how you're currently perceived. If you haven't established yourself as a squeaky tight player up till now, then your package raise will have no impact; it will be treated as just another raise from a player who has been raising, well, as much as everyone else. In fact if you think about it, there's no inconsistency at all in making a raise with a junk hand if you're already seen as aggressive. It's right in keeping with your image, and it's likely to be greeted by a lot of ho-hum calls. So, really, what's the point?

Here's the way to think about raising with package hands. Like a pitcher establishing his fastball, you first establish yourself as tight by raising only with premium hands (or not getting involved at all). Once you've got your foes trained to the notion that you only raise with great cards, you can add in your package hands, as a pitcher would mix in his curveball. Just as the curve works better once the fastball has been established, your complication raises will work better once you have your tightness well vetted. Again, if you don't have the right (tight) image, a raise here is neither inconsistent nor unexpected; in short, it's a waste.

Finally there's this. A lot of hands qualify as package hands, *but not all package hands qualify as raising hands.* For myself, I favor middle suited connectors, specifically 9-8 and 8-7 as my package hands—but I don't raise with every one I get. Usually I pick two suits and add only those four hands into my package. If the game is such that I can play more liberally, I'll add a third suit. If the game is frisky, such that I want to avoid reckless adventures, I'll drop a suit, or drop my package play altogether. In this way, I fine-tune the amount of inconsistency and unpredictability that I'm injecting into my game—which amount is further shaped by my table image, the quality of my opposition, relative stack sizes, and so on.

Do the same for yourself. Pick out a handful of package hands—only a handful—and add them into your mix. Candidates include smaller pairs and lesser wheelhouse combinations like Q-J and K-T. If you're the sort of player who plays too predictably preflop, it's a useful way to throw 'em a curve.

Further to this, just think about the impact—the meta-impact, if you will—that such conscious decisions will have on your game. Instead of lurching into a hand with no clearer plan than to see what the cards may bring, you have a series of if-then routines and subroutines that inform and guide your play. To a measure, this takes the guesswork out of poker, and anything that takes out the guesswork is, I guess, a good idea.

TOP/TOP ON THE FLOP

We love our top pair/top kickers. When we hold two big cards and the flop comes top/top, we feel like we're on top of the world. But here's a sad fact of hands like top pair, top kicker in NLHE: It's hard to win big pots with them. This seems counterintuitive, I know, and maybe a little unfair. After all, if you've waited patiently for A-K and then gotten the flop you were looking for, K-x-x or A-x-x, you feel like you deserve to get paid for your patience. But let's look at those flops of K-x-x or A-x-x. What sort of hands are you likely to face if you bet and get called? Straight draws and flush draws or, worse, two pair or sets. All other holdings, underpairs, runner-runner draws, and pure rags, will (or should) fold. It's not that hard to put someone on top/top, after all, and absent a good reason to stay, most folks will scram. A big bet on the flop, then, invites action only from hands that have a decent chance of getting ahead or being ahead already.

Does this mean you shouldn't protect your top/top? Not at all. A bet is called for here, and a bet should be made. But be sure to think past the flop to the turn and the river—have a plan for the hand, right? This foresight will give you a choice of paths to take, each of which has merit, and each of which allows you to control the size of the pot and shape how the hand develops. By switching among them, you can increase your unpredictability without sacrificing your edge. You can also avoid the typical trap of top/top: winning a small pot or losing a big one.

The conventional approach to top/top is to *bet big on the flop and, if no scare card comes on the turn, bet big again*. Against weak, tight players this is the way to go because they'll surrender without a fight, which is fine. If your foes are weak and loose, you're still okay because you can bet big enough to give them incorrect odds to call. Or so you hope. Suppose there's $100 in the pot and you're in there with top/top against three deep-stacked Wallies. It's checked to you. If you bet, say, $75, you'll be giving the first caller incorrect odds to draw, but should she happen to call it will open the door to the rest of the field, each of whom will be getting more and more favorable math. You might find yourself in there with top/top against three callers in a pot so big you can't bet them off it on the turn.

And, of course, they might not be on a draw. Someone out there might have two pair or a set, in which case here's what you're going to see: check-call on the flop, check-raise (and raise *big*) on the turn. When that happens, you're going to be dangling off a cliff. You'll either have to let your top/top go or else plunge down with it. Since you won't know whether your loose, weak foes are on draws or big hands, you'd rather not face that hard choice if you can avoid it. You might want to consider plan B.

In this scenario, you *bet bigger on the flop to thin the field, but then check the turn to keep the pot small*. This approach has two merits. First, it keeps you out of the jaws of a lurking check-raise. Second, it creates a pot you can value bet—for the right price—on the river. Again, let's put you on top/top with $100 in the pot against three deep-stacked callers. Again it's checked to you, and again you bet. Only this time, you bet the pot, $100. This inspires the first Wally to fold, which in turn inspires the second Wally to fold. Only the third Wally calls and you get to the turn with a smaller pot, but also a smaller field.

Now think about checking the turn. Yes, you're giving a free card, and we've heard that's taboo—but you're also controlling the size of the pot. The alternatives to checking here are betting small (in which case you might give the right odds to draw or invite a raise), or betting big (in which case you'll either win without a fight, which is fine, or face a big raise, which is not). While it's true that you won't always want to give a free card, remember two things: One, the free card will most often not help someone who's either trailing you in the hand or on a draw; and two, you're mixing up your play and therefore distorting their picture of you.

The beauty of betting big on the flop to thin the field and then checking the turn to retard the growth of the pot is that it delivers you to the river in position to extract extra value from your remaining foe. Recalling that you checked the turn, if the river comes bricky, you may very well look like you're on a busted draw and a naked steal attempt. You certainly won't look like you're on top/top, since checking top/top on the turn is a *very* uncharacteristic play. So then your foe may call you with second pair, or maybe even her own busted draw. This was your plan for the hand all along. This was why you bet the flop and checked the turn: to extract maximum value for minimum risk with your top/top, a hand that is at once strong and strangely vulnerable.

Plan C is a bit more direct. You go for a *check-raise on the flop to win the pot right there.* Many people confuse a hand that's ahead with one that's a lock. That's why they're content to bet small-to-medium on the flop and small-to-medium on the turn. They think they're milking their foes, but actually they're just pricing people into the pot. Your top/top is a good hand, but it's not a cinch to win. One way to play it is to protect it with the force of most, or all, of your chips.

In this scenario, you're in early position with several players behind you, including one frisky speeder you know to be capable of betting with a second-best hand and/or a draw. You check, hoping he bets, which he obligingly does. It's called around to you and you check-raise a prohibitively large amount. You want to drive off all the draws. Really, you want to drive off everyone. The plan for this hand is *win it on the flop, full stop.*

There will be times when the plan goes awry, such as when no one downstream takes the bait and bets the flop for you. In that case, you have given a free card and if the turn card is scary you may be stuck with check-calling or check-folding. On the other hand, if Speedy bets his second-best hand or his draw, you can blow him off the hand with a big bet, and collect extra chips.

Which of these is the best plan for the hand? *No se.* It depends on the number of foes you're up against, and their makeup, not to mention your table image and position, depth of stacks (or tournament situation), and a dozen other factors. I'm not here to preach one play over another, for all of them can work and, equally, all of them can go horribly wrong. I'm here to preach flexibility and forward planning. If you find yourself with top/top and know that you have some options on how to play it, you deal yourself two edges: card edge and skill edge. If you always play this hand the same way—bludgeon the pot with bets—you have only the advantage of your cards, and that's often not nearly enough.

SNATCH A COOKIE

Do you bluff enough? Many people don't, because they're so afraid of being busted . . . like it'll go down in their permanent record or something. They'd rather never bluff, or bluff only when they seem like a lock not to get called, than to risk—let's call it what it is—the shame of getting caught. But Annie Duke, World Series of Poker champ and all-around poker goddess, has something to say on the subject. "If you don't get caught with your hand in the cookie jar every now and then," she notes "you're not playing the game right." Let's take a look now at the art of cookie snatching, and integrate it into our growing matrix of unpredictability.

As we know, there are two kinds of deception in poker: bluffing and trapping. From a psychological point of view, most players find it much easier to trap than to bluff, because they trap with confidence. They know they have a winning hand and they're just trying to extract maximum value. Should they fail to do so, they feel that all they've lost is a little extra profit. (This line of reasoning misses the essential point that lost profit hurts the bottom line every bit as much as squandered bets, but let's let that go for now.) To bluff, on the other hand, is to risk chips that one could just as easily keep in one's stack. And it's not just the chips. Many players fear losing . . . face. There seems to be something so *schoolyard* about having a bluff snapped off. *You thought you could get away with* that*?! Ha! Sucker!* Bluffing, then, is scary for many players. Is it scary for you? Take a moment to examine your state of mind on the subject. Project yourself into a bluffing situation and prospect your feelings there. I'm not saying you will, but if you discover an emotional block standing between you and the act of bluffing, understand that you will not be able to bluff effectively until you have addressed and removed this block.

>>

Bluffing is a rush for me, no doubt. I love the secret, smug satisfaction of getting someone to fold a winner. I might even say, "Nice laydown" (and if you're playing against me you might come to recognize this as a tell). But bluffing scares me, too, no doubt. If it looks like I'll get caught, I'll more likely back

away than follow through, even at the cost of chips invested
in the pot, or in the bluff, so far. When I get caught, I feel it—
I can feel it even now just by writing about it—right down to
the soles of my feet, which, strangely, sweat whenever I take a
big hit on a big bluff.

So for me personally there's a healthy dose of approach/
avoidance conflict when it comes to bluffing. I love when it
works, but hate when it fails—hate it so much that I bluff less
than I should. But Annie says we can't hate when bluffs fail,
that we must embrace failed bluffs as part of the price of
poker. You're no doubt familiar with the concept of "advertis-
ing," and the notion that we have to show some bluffs from
time to time in order to get paid off on our real, good, or real
good hands. Intellectually we understand that; emotionally,
there's still perhaps a rock in our gut. What do we do about
that?

One thing we could do—man, you're gonna hate this—is
to *try to get caught on purpose*. It's ridiculous, I know; possibly
the most inane idea I've had in poker since the Suicide Raise
Scenario.[2] Nevertheless, one way to deal with emotional blocks
is to confront them head-on and shatter them, even at the price
of a few chips. If you're game, then, the next time you go to
play poker, tell yourself in advance that on a given hand (the
twenty-third, say) you're going to run a stone bluff through
the field, just to see how it feels. Tell yourself you won't mind
getting caught because that's the point of the exercise: to see
how it feels to get caught with that hand in that jar. I think
you'll find—and yes, I have tried this myself—that the red-
faced pain of getting caught is mitigated by the pride of having done what you set out to do. It's strange, I know, and

2. The Suicide Raise Scenario, if you don't know, suggests buying into
a low limit poker game and raising every chance you get until you
either go broke or double through. It's (usually) a colossal waste of
money, but it does have the salutary effect of modeling hyper-
aggressive poker play.

potentially costly, but it's a good way to scrape the barnacles off your will to bluff.

Meanwhile, back at inconsistent and unpredictable, we're still faced with the issue of mixing bluffs into our play. Assuming we've settled the emotional issue and can now bluff at will, the question remains: *When will we bluff?* Liberating as it may be to experience failure, that's not something we want to make a habit of, so let's avoid situations where bluffs are highly unlikely to succeed. Instead, let's hunt for circumstances where bluffing and not bluffing may be nearly equally correct, and make sure that we're on the bluffing side of the ledger a sufficient amount of the time.

There are times when bluffing is simply a waste of time, money, and image. Say you've raised preflop with 8♣-8♠ and gotten three callers. That's too many callers for this hand, as it now must hit to win unless you can bluff successfully. But the flop comes K♥-Q♥-T♥, putting three to a flush and three to a straight—not to mention three wheelhouse cards—on board. That's the sort of flop that hits everyone's hand. Who's going to fold if you bet? Not a flush draw or straight draw or straight flush draw. Not top/top, nor two pair, sets, or those who flopped made hands and now look with delicious anticipation for the chance to trap. If you have reason to believe that you have the best hand (unlikely, to my eyes) then by all means go ahead and bet; otherwise, save your chips for a more . . . shall we say . . . organic bluffing opportunity.

The *scare card bluff* is one such organic opportunity. You'll recognize it as a relative of adopting orphans, and it's a move that can be profitably made against a wide variety of opponents, provided your table image is correct. In this instance, you're looking for a flop that has not much more going for it than a draw. For example, say you've limped into a pot holding Big Maxx, K♣-Q♣, and now see a flop of 9-8-7 rainbow. Someone bets at it, and you figure her for A-9 or A-8. If your image is thoughtful/tight, and you're thus known as someone who doesn't get far out of line, you can call a bet here, for a king or a queen on the turn will probably give you the best hand, and a six or a ten will give you the chance to fake the straight. Folding certainly wouldn't be wrong here—you only have overcard outs right now—but in the name of inconsistency (and having a plan for the hand) you can stick around and see what happens next.

It's worth noting that when you include programmed bluffs like this into your calculations, you can occasionally turn otherwise prohibitive pot odds in your favor. Let's say that in the example we're using there's $100 in the pot and the bettor leads at it for $50. Now there's $150 in the pot, and if you call $50, you'll be getting a 3–1 ROI (return on investment). If all you have going are your overcards, assuming them to be good, you only have six outs, meaning that you're about 7–1 against hitting on the turn. You have nowhere near correct pot odds and could correctly fold. But if you include the tens and sixes as *phantom outs*—cards that would complete your hand if you had the hand you're representing—you suddenly have 14 outs and you're about 2.5–1 against hitting on the turn. *Mirable visu,* you've got correct odds to call. But only if you're willing to bluff when the scare card comes. Then it's gut-check time. However, many people find it easier to follow through on their bluffs if they plan them in advance in this way. Further, once you've nominated a card as "helpful" to your hand (or phantom hand as the case may be) you tend to bet it with more confidence. In your gut, you feel like you've hit your hand. This emotional certitude lends extra credence to your bluff, for you exude an authentic subconscious "I have a straight" air, which many foes will interpret as a tell, and get away from their hand.

Two things worth noting. First, keep in mind that the scare card bluff works best in the event of flops of indifferent present quality. While a flop like K-Q-J offers the same straight possibilities as 9-8-7, it offers considerable other high card possibilities, making it less likely that foes who have connected with the flop will be eager to get away from their hands. Second, as with all bluffs, the scare card bluff works best against one or at

most two opponents, for the simple reason that the more players you confront, the more likely you are to face someone who
actually has a hand. In other words—and this is key to successful bluffing—

BLUFF THE FEW,
NOT THE MANY.

For an even more aggressive approach to the scare card
bluff, instead of calling the flop, go ahead and raise. If you're
in position, this will often get the betting checked to you on
the turn. Should you hit one of your outs or phantom outs,
you can go ahead and bet, but if a brick comes, you have the
luxury of checking. This may actually sell your bluff more effectively, for your foes may very well interpret your raise on
the flop to have been a *foreclosure raise,* a raise made by a drawing hand for the purpose of stalling the action and getting a
free card on the turn. In this case, a ten or a six on the river
will look very convincingly like the card you needed, leaving
you free to bluff at the pot for the second time in the hand.

The scare card bluff, in sum, is a tactic you can use in situations where folding, calling, or raising could all be correct. By
selecting among these options, you inject flexibility into your
play without sacrificing the overall quality of your approach.

Some players are not content to bluff situationally. Recalling
the *Crazy Ivan* move from *The Hunt for Red October* (wherein
submarine commander Marko Ramius made a sudden, unexpected maneuver at a predetermined time), they like to plan
their bluffs in advance. There are a number of ways to go
about this. Like Ramius, you could use the clock, scheduling
your bluffs for five past the hour, say. Believe me, it's an un-
usually attentive foe who can detect that pattern and use it
against you. Another approach is to select certain hands—
pocket fives or K♠-x♠, say—and play them as if they were
pocket aces. Note that you can easily adjust your bluffing fre-

quency just by changing the number of Crazy Ivans or, if you prefer, *faux rockets* you care to name. The merit of this method is that your preselected hands will take on a changed character in your mind. As in the case of hitting your phantom outs, these hands may end up seeming authentically strong and betworthy to you, since you're looking for them as eagerly as you're looking for real pocket aces. You'll be able to follow through much more convincingly, and therefore much more effectively, on your bluff, because it won't seem entirely like a bluff to you. The danger of this method (it's only fair to mention the danger) is that you may find yourself bluffing at exactly the wrong time: in early position against savvy, frisky foes, say, or butting heads with Wallies who can't be driven from the pot. So have a couple of Crazy Ivans in mind when you enter a session, but never feel obliged to run bluffs with them if the circumstances aren't conducive.

If you find Crazy Ivan to be a little too lockstep (or just too crazy) for your taste, then let your bluffing opportunities be guided by others' perception of you. In other words, *surf your image*. Recognize that the longer you go without raising, the more likely is your raise to be treated by others as a credible threat. If your image is right, your foes will often give you a free pass at the pot. Think about it: You haven't voluntarily entered a pot for 45 minutes; now, suddenly, you open for a big raise. Doesn't that action seem consistent with the play of a rock who finally found a hand? In your opponents' eyes, you're much more likely to be betting a quality holding than a stone bluff. And even if they have half a hand, they'll often fold because they expect a tighty like you to go back to sleep for another 45 minutes anyhow, and they don't want to give you action in the rare moments when you seem to have come awake.

Needless to say, this is why it doesn't pay to be too tight in NLHE. Yes, you'll win the infrequent uncontested blinds, but you'll never get action on your good hands. Nevertheless, sometimes the cards tell us what to do, and if your cards—7-2,

8-4, jackthree, jackthree, jackthree—tell you to fold often enough, you'll find yourself with a super snug image whether you like it or not. Like it! It's an opportunity to bluff and, as I said, almost a free pass to steal. If you've been wandering in the card desert sufficiently long, go ahead and tell yourself that the next hand is a raising hand, no matter what. Should you get callers, look for the sort of flop that tight players love, one rich in aces and kings. If that flop doesn't come, you'll have trouble essaying a bluff, since it won't mesh with the image you have of someone who waits for good cards. Of course, there's always the possibility that you'll *hit* your bluff hand, in which case you have the opportunity to do damage to someone's stack, and also reveal the ragged hand with which you raised. And yes, this type of bluff is related to adding package hands into the mix when your image is right. The only difference is that you're not relying on the right cards so much as the right situation in which to send forth a bluff.

Further to the notion of surfing your image, remember that your image is always somewhere, and you should adjust your bluffing frequency according to where it is right now. If you're perceived as tight, bluff more; if you're perceived as loose, bluff less. This is Poker 101 stuff, I know, but it bears noting just the same. If you're fortunate enough to hit a bluff hand and show it down as a winner, there's just no way you can turn around and bluff again for a while. Everyone saw you win with 9-7; if you raise again soon, they're not likely to credit you with a raiseworthy hand.

Constantly monitor your image. Before each deal, ask yourself, *How do my foes perceive me now?* Many top pros speak of intentionally changing gears, from laid-back to aggressive or the other way around, but image is often a pendulum that swings on its own, guided by how we're running, the relative strength of our foes, and stack size. If you've been playing a lot of hands and are perceived as loose, bluffing opportunities are few and far between. (An exception: If you've been playing loose and winning a lot, bluffing opportunities actually increase because no one wants to mess with you.) If you've been playing tight, or if the cards have been forcing you to take a backseat to the action, you should be looking for the bluff opportunities that your image is handing you.

In general, the realm of bluffing is a fruitful one for reducing the predictability of your play. Since it's not always right to bluff and not always right *not* to bluff, variation is not only called for but actually mandated here.

OTHER OPPORTUNITIES

These are not, of course, the only poker situations that offer multiple correct courses of action. If you go looking for them, your own experience will reveal to you many other "flex" opportunities. How do you play pocket jacks? Do you always raise in late position but call in early position? The other way around? Do you always call with your draws? Fold them? Raise them? For reasons of habit or confirmation bias ("this way worked before so it'll probably work now") we fall into patterns of play that our attentive foes can easily decipher and decode. To throw them off the scent, it's vital that we throw misdirection into the mix. Again, this need not mean playing incorrectly for the sake of sheer deception; rather, it means playing creatively, choosing among correct paths, and varying the choices you make.

It's worth building a collection of "option play" situations, writing them down in your poker notebook, and keeping them in mind so you can put them to work. If you mix up your play in situations when more than one play is correct, you'll blend sufficient unpredictability and inconsistency into your game that you'll become suitably hard to read—ultimately the sort of player that you'd hate to have to play against.

PART II
♣ ♠ ♦ ♥

A GOOD DAY AT PLAY

♧ ♤ ◇ ♡

6

THE PERFECT CRIME
PLANNING TOOL

The structure of fixed limit poker has been so popular for so long because the cost of bad play is, well, limited. Here's the performance chart for a typical unsuccessful limit hold'em player.

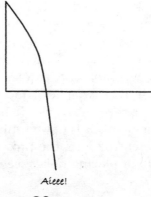

Rats.

Now here's the performance chart for the same player in no limit Texas hold'em.

Aieee!

As you can see from this crude illustration, it's much more costly to be a bad no limit hold'em player than to be a bad limit hold'em player. Because NLHE is such an unforgiving game, we need to be ready to win every time we sit down to play, for errors that would cost us a big bet or two in a limit hold'em cash game will take us off our whole stack in no limit. These errors—momentary lapses of reason that cause us to make ill-considered big calls or run ill-considered big bluffs—represent a gaping hole in most people's play. It is therefore required of us to enter every no limit cash game in a state of sufficient intellectual rigor to avert and avoid catastrophic mental meltdowns throughout our playing day.

Before you sit down to play . . . before you even head out to play . . . the first thing you want to do is check your head and make sure you're in the right frame of mind to engage in the powerful, precise thinking that topflight poker play demands. It's easy to get careless on this score. For instance, I often find myself driving in Los Angeles from point A to point B on a route that takes me past my favorite local cardrooms. Sometimes on the merest pretext—to wait out traffic, say, or just because it's there—I'll drop in for an unpremeditated poker session. These sessions can be hazardous because I'm often not in my "poker head," but still mentally connected to whatever business was taking me from point A to point B in the first place.

Want to hear an even worse example? At various times I've been color commentator for televised poker broadcasts, and these broadcasts inevitably originate in casinos. If there's any lengthy delay or hole in the schedule, such as technical difficulties or even just lunch, I've been known to scamper off to the nearest poker table, looking to see a few flops and score a quick win. Or even not score a quick win. Sometimes it's clear to me that winning is far less important than seeing those flops, scratching the well-known itch to play poker. You don't have to tell me that this is flawed thinking. I know it's flawed. Yet, as is so often the case, the prospect of spending even an unprofitable hour playing poker seems more appealing to me

than the prospect of spending that hour doing almost anything else.

Like the sign says,

THE WORST DAY OF POKER
IS BETTER THAN
THE BEST DAY AT WORK.

Like the other sign says,

THE PROBLEM IS NOT: *PLAYING POKER.*
THE PROBLEM IS: *NOT PLAYING POKER.*

Has it ever happened to you? Have you ever found yourself
backing into a poker game, or cramming a poker session into
the corners of your otherwise occupied time? Can you recount
to yourself such a circumstance and articulate the feelings (ea-
gerness, impatience, maybe even guilt?) that accompanied the
experience?

>>

Online poker is even more problematic because it's so
damned accessible. One minute you're watching TV or reading a good book and the next you've jumped into a game online. Again, with no premeditation and no mental preparation,
we can hardly expect to bring our most effective mind-set to
the game. Yet we find ourselves there again and again. We'll
see some titan of the World Poker Tour run a naked bluff for
all his chips with T-4 offsuit and think, "Well, that looks like
fun." Then off we'll dash to our computers, all enthusiastic and
avid, but not really ready to play well.

To protect myself generally against wandering into a poker
game unprepared, I use the *perfect crime planning tool,* so called

because it requires that I have sufficient *means, motive,* and *opportunity* before I sit down to play in any online or realworld cash game.

MEANS

Do I have enough money to play the game properly? Is the amount of money available to me adequate for the game I plan to play in? And even if my bankroll is adequate in absolute terms, how is my head? There are times when having the money and feeling comfortable about putting that money into play are two very different things. I measure my means against the state of my poker game. If I feel like I can play well and meet the challenge of bigger buy in games, then I'll set higher ceilings for myself. If I'm back on my heels (as we all are from time to time) I'm more likely to play smaller. I'm keen to protect my bankroll. Sometimes I know I'm just there to "hack around," play some poker, pass the time of day. Recognizing my own frivolity, I limit my financial exposure by playing at the low end of my cash game range.

I want to stress this point, because I think it's one of the great unspoken truths of poker: We often play when we know our hearts aren't in it. In a perfect world, this wouldn't be the case. In a perfect world, we would limit our poker forays to the times when our minds are laser sharp and our commitment to excellence unwavering. Well, the last time I checked, it wasn't a perfect world (as evidenced by the facts that doughnuts are still fattening and tequila makes you fall down), so it seems to me that the least we can do is acknowledge our atavistic urges, and protect ourselves against them by playing small when we know our heads aren't right.

All of which begs the question, what is adequate funding for today's NLHE cash games?

Below you'll see a chart of available NLHE games in the places I play—the cavernous card barns of Southern California.

The expression *min/max* refers to the condition of a mandated buy in; in these cases exactly $40, $100 or $200, no more, no less. Min/max buy in conditions are typical in many NLHE games because they keep big money from dominating and destabilizing the game.

BUY IN	BLINDS
$40 min/max	50 cents–$1
$100 min/max	$2–$3
$200 min/max	$3–$5
$300 min, $500 max	$5–$5
$500 min, no max	$5–$10
$1,000 min, no max	$10–$20

At one time or another, I might play in any of these games, except the $40 buy in game. (Nor would I recommend that anyone except the greenest no limit newbie play that low, for the house take is proportionally so high that the game is virtually unbeatable.) All other things being equal (which of course they're not), which one should I choose? Though others have more sophisticated formulas for money management, I use this simple rule of thumb: I never put more than 10 percent of my bankroll into play in any one game at any one time. Using this approach, I figure I'll have to get really hammered a lot of times in a row in order to lose my bankroll and—given my 10 percent rule of thumb—I will have dropped down to a smaller game long before that happens.[3]

Let's say I've got a $5,000 bankroll. Ten percent of that bankroll is adequate to buy me into either the $300–$500 game or the $500 min, no max game. There are arguments both for and against buying in for the minimum in a no max buy in game, and we'll get to those arguments shortly. For now let's

3. Annie Duke proposes even stricter strictures, and recommends never putting more than 5 percent to 8 percent of your bankroll in play. As she's a good deal smarter than I am, you can certainly go with her guidelines on this.

just assume that I consider $500 enough for the game with $5 and $10 blinds. And let's say that I lose my buy in. Now my bankroll is $4,500, and 10 percent of that, $450, will no longer fund me in the $500 minimum game. (Yes, I know there are such things as short buy ins, but I don't recommend them; if you're so imperiled by your bankroll, your mind-set, or your opposition as to want to limit your risk in a game, you'd be much better served to go find a different game.) Given my rule of thumb, I have to drop down a level or two—and I'm more likely to drop down two than one. As a matter of personal preference, I'd rather be generously funded for a smaller game than barely bankrolled for a bigger one.

You can use this sliding scale for whatever games happen to be available where you are. Twenty-five-dollar buy in games abound online, for instance, and a $250 online bankroll is adequate for them. If your bankroll drops below $100, though, you'll have to drop, too, all the way down to the $5 or $10 buy in games. It may seem to you that playing for such paltry sums is not worth your time of day—and you may be right— but playing in a game too big for your bankroll is a recipe for disaster. One spike of negative fluctuation and you're all the way down to the felt. Then you'll be playing in the tiny games anyhow, as a matter of necessity. Why not make the drop when it's your *choice* to do so, when the issue is protecting— not rebuilding—your bankroll?

This 10 percent rule works the other way as well. If you score a big win, you can move up to a bigger game. But remember that just because you *can* move up doesn't mean you *must* move up. Means alone are not the only test for a poker game. How's your head? How's the competition? Don't assume that double the buy in means double the profit for you.

Be aware that ego may impact your choices. To play in low buy in games seems somehow demeaning when you've been playing higher. And if you've been running well and find yourself sufficiently funded for bigger games, pride may put you into them, just so you can feel like the poker juggernaut you think (and fervently hope) you are. These ego considerations are absolutely real—and absolutely irrelevant. Until you can dispassionately match your aspiration to your bankroll, and not the other way around, you don't have adequate means— mental means, that is—to play the game correctly.

MOTIVE

To have the proper motive for poker means to have the *desire* and the *ability* to play well from the first hand to the last. Just as a relatively poor state of mind is an argument for playing small, an absolutely rotten state of mind is an absolute argument for doing something altogether else. We think of discipline in terms of not playing certain hands, but discipline in a larger sense means not playing at all. Some pros or would-be pros have trouble with this concept. They believe that they have to "put in their hours" whether they're feeling up to the task or not. This may be the most specious rationalization I've ever heard for playing poker. If you're not right, you're not right; and if you're not right, then "putting in your hours" will only cost you money. Who needs the grief?

To clarify this point, let me borrow from my experience as a writer. Just like professional poker players, writers have to put in their hours; otherwise, the job doesn't get done, the money doesn't get earned, and the bills don't get paid. But I know from long years at my craft that some days I'm just in the wrong place to write effectively. I call this "cheese brain" and I know that when it kicks in, not only will I not be productive, I'll actually be counterproductive, lose all critical faculties, and do damage to whatever I happen to be working on at the time. It's the same with poker. If your mind-set is crap, your results will be crap, too.

So I'm careful to avoid playing poker whenever I'm tired,

sick, jet-lagged, drunk, impatient, distracted, or mad at the
world. You, I assume, are careful to avoid playing poker whenever you are . . .

>>

Again, this is discipline, and this discipline is not easy to
come by. The mind, with its crafty capacity for rationalization, will reason thus:

*I'm in a sucky mood. I know I'm in a sucky mood, and if I
were playing poker in this mood, I could hardly expect to do
well. However (!) playing poker always makes me feel better,
so if I go play poker, even though I'm currently in a sucky
mood, I'll probably leave the sucky mood behind as soon as I
sit down to play. Then I'll play great, win a lot of money, and
never be in a sucky mood again.*

May I just say . . . *yeah, right.*
We talked earlier about risk averse and risk affined thinking; how a risk averse player will look for a reason not to get
involved, while a risk affined player will look for a reason to
jump in. Both players are victims of subjective reality, filtering
the facts through the prism of their desire. Likewise, when we
contemplate the choice of playing or not playing poker, we
run the risk of weighting the facts in such a way as to give us
the result we wanted all along.
Sure I'm tired, but some coffee'll cure that.
Sure I'm drunk, but I know I'm drunk so I'll compensate.
Sure I'm ill, but what the hell?
Before you go to play poker, every time you play poker,
stop to check and make sure that your motivation is sound.
Make sure you're playing because you've made the conscious
decision that it's the right and the profitable thing to do.
Don't let self-indulgence influence your thinking. Above all,

see things as they are. Be prepared to ask, and frankly answer, questions like these:

- Am I adequately rested?
- Am I happy?
- Am I tranquil?
- Am I patient?
- Am I physically well?
- Am I "in it to win it"?

Or the questions crucial to you.

>>

If you can answer yes to these questions, then consider yourself cleared for takeoff—all systems go for poker. If you can't answer yes, just don't play. It's hard, I know, but it's a skill vital to your long-term success. Per Mike Caro, the money you don't lose spends the same as the money you win.

OPPORTUNITY

Even when you have enough money and enough motivation to play poker correctly, you might not have enough time. Trying to cram a few hands of hold'em into a small available window is likely to leave you feeling rushed . . . and unlikely to leave you with a win. I can think of several reasons why this would be the case, and I'm sure that you can, too.

>>

Did you mention the problem of patience? If you know you have only an hour to play, you'll force the action, trying to squeeze profit out of marginal or even clearly negative situations. To take one obvious example, you'll call with your draws even though the pot odds don't warrant, for you may feel that this is the only hit-to-win opportunity you'll have during this session. You came to play, you'll tell yourself, thereby justifying all sorts of unprofitable hand speculations. You'll force the action, figuring that you don't have time to wait for better opportunities. Of course this is an ass-backward way to think about poker—we should be thinking only of playing correctly, not of booking a win in this, that, or any session—but it's a common train of thought for players locked into a short session.

Then there's the matter of knowing our foes. In a long session, we can take the time to figure out who's frisky and straightforward, risk affined and risk averse. In a short session, we blunder blindly into confrontations with foes we don't know. Here I am, trying to bet Joe Beets off a pot, and after he calls me down with bottom pair (and wins!) the guy next to me whispers, "You can't bluff that guy. He never folds." Yeah, it would've been nice to know that beforehand. And there's no reason I couldn't have known—except that the pressure of a short session forced me into action before I had my reads dialed in.

Take your time. If you don't have time to play a thoughtful, patient, well-reasoned session of poker, don't play at all.

Even if you have enough time, you might not be able to find the right game. Here, again, ego may color perception. We look at the games available to us and—filtering reality through pride—figure there's not one we can't beat. That's gogglebox nonsense—the worst kind of nonsense there is. Of *course* there are games you can't beat, and if you can't admit this fact to yourself you run the risk of putting yourself into the wrong game over and over and over again. This is true whether we're playing online or in the realworld. For instance, I love playing heads-up online. I figure I'm pretty good at it, and I'll happily go head-to-head with almost anyone. *Almost.* There are some players out there—I know who they are, for I've made extensive book on them—that I just can't handle. Given a choice between tangling with these monsters and not playing at all, I simply *must* opt for not playing at all.

You might experience this same phenomenon in a real-world casino where the lists are long for the game at your chosen level or buy in, but nonexistent for bigger games. The desire to get into action *now* will cause you to forget your bankroll limitations, and your pride will tell you that the players aren't *that* much better than you. Shall we spin out this nightmare scenario to its sad conclusion? You go first.

>>

Now I'll take a whack.

Okay, so I have my eye on the $3 and $5 blind $200 min/max game. It's full of players I've faced before and know I can best. The list for that game is a mile long, though, while on the other hand, the $5 and $10 blind game has a seat open right now. Forgetting for the moment that my bankroll is nowhere near big enough to suffer the swings of this game (which I conveniently do forget 'cause I *really* want to play), I decide to take that seat. Though everyone in the game has more than $5,000 in front of him, I can't muster more than a grand. Therefore I'll be short stacked from the get-go. I remember the immortal words of, well, me . . .

SHORT MONEY = SCARED MONEY.

And you know what? It's true: I am playing with scared money. But that's okay, I tell myself, 'cause I have *a plan!* I'm going to play just incredibly tight until a seat comes available in the small game. I'll restrict myself to premium hands and in this way limit my exposure. And who knows? If I get lucky and catch some cards, I might even book a win before I move back down to my comfort zone.

Naturally my observant opponents realize where I'm at. They know I'm uncomfortable, and if the short buy in doesn't give me away, the snugness of my play sure does. So I fold, fold, fold, fold along for a while, and then I pick up pocket queens in late position. Of course I should raise, but of course I don't, because this is a big game, an aggressive game, and I'm afraid to bet my hand. The small blind folds and the big blind checks and we see a flop of 7-3-3. I go ahead and bet, figuring to win the pot right here, only to face a monster reraise. I know nothing about my foe and, since she got a free look from the big blind, I also know nothing about her hand. Nevertheless, I lapse into an *I know that she knows that I know that she knows* evaluation of this orphan flop, and conclude that I'm being bullied by overcards. Sigh. Turns out she has a three.

Oh, man!

Where did my stack go?

And what was I trying to accomplish in the first place? To kill some time and not lose any money while waiting for the game of my choice. Goodness! I could have done the same thing with a crossword puzzle! Look, if we don't have the patience to sit and wait for a favorable game, how can we possibly have the patience to play in that game correctly?

We can't. Just can't.

But let's assume that we do have that patience. Let's further assume that our means, motive, and opportunity all pass appropriate muster. Now, at last, we're called to a seat in a game where the buy in is right and the lineup's not too tough. We're here, we're hot, and we're ready to rock.

Let the games, as they say, begin.

7

BREATHING IN

If you're playing in a fixed buy in NLHE game, you have no choice about how much money to put into play. You just plunk down your cash and away you go. If the buy in is spread ($300 to $500, say) or unlimited (minimum $500, no maximum), then you'll have to think about how much money you want to put on the table and why. As I said earlier, there are strong arguments for buying in short and other strong arguments for buying in long. Let's look at these arguments now.

The short buy in limits your exposure. It gives you the potential (if luck and your own skill make it so) of building a big stack without risking a similar amount in return. This works best for players who are long on patience and short on creativity. With a short buy in, you're planning to sit tight until you have good cards or great cards, then get your money in and hope your hand holds up. If it's your intention to mix it up in a lot of pots, you simply need more bullets in your gun. Otherwise, if you make a couple of moves and don't connect, before you know it you'll have a stack so small that your only legitimate move is an all-in push. At that point you're waiting for big tickets and watching the blinds go by.

The big buy in increases your risk, but also your flexibility. If you know that it's in your nature to play a lot of hands, or that it's your intention to take over the table, or that the players you're facing are particularly loose and weak, then your large (or maximum) buy in will give you extra room to maneuver. Particularly if you don't mind big swings, you want to put a lot of money on the table so that you can make big bets with big hands.

Another consideration is the size of the stacks you face. If the money is very deep on the table, you must either go very deep yourself, in order to put yourself on an equal footing, or opt for the minimum buy in with the intention of building your stack by degrees until it's large enough to become a meaningful weapon. The former path is not always possible. Consider a $300 to $500 spread buy in game that's been going on for many hours. Players have come and gone, and the eight or nine you now face all have stacks well over $1,000. The largest is $3,500 and the average is two grand. But the most you can buy in for is $500, which means that you'll start out as the short stack, with all that implies in terms of having to play selective/defensive poker. Since $500 isn't enough to put you on an equal footing, you might as well just buy in for $300. Your strategy is exactly the same, but your exposure is 40 percent less. This, by the way, is one circumstance where short money isn't necessarily scared money, since the rules of the game constrain your buy in. You're not scared; you're just following the rules.

Do pause to consider whether you're even in the right game. While it's possible to make a short stack work in a game where the money all around you is deep, ask yourself how the money got so deep in the first place. True, these might be the luckiest ducks who ever drew breath, but it's more likely that some or all of these players are running well and playing well, which will make it that much harder for you to gain a toehold in the game. Take a look around the room. Is there another game where the money is less deep, and where your buy in will give you a stronger relative position? It often happens that inertia or laziness plants our butts in the first available seat, even if the game is unfavorable and we *know* it's unfavorable.

For this reason, it's a good idea to keep your name on the sign-up lists for various games. It would only be a matter of luck if you landed in the softest game in the room, so keep your eye peeled for a softer one. I recognize that you might be playing in a small cardroom, where your choice of games is severely restricted (in which case you might have to default to Plan B: don't play). Still, always keep in mind the importance of game selection. In a sense, it forgives a multitude of sins. If you've chosen the right game, you can play wrong hands and get away with it.

If it helps you to practice patience while you're waiting for a seat, recognize that every minute of waiting gives you a free look at all available games and a chance to pick your best target of opportunity. There are many easy ways to tell whether a given game is good or not. We've already considered the relative depth of money in play. I do consider deep money to be a warning sign: *Someone* must be doing *something* right. It is argued that deep money should be attacked and not avoided, because, well, there's lots of it and it's there for the (attempted) taking. While I admire the confidence of this, I'm never concerned about there being "enough" money on the table. If I bust a bunch of small stacks, I know that those seats will be filled with other players (or the game will break and I'll have to go home, poor me). The relevant factor, then, is not the amount of money currently in play at the table, but rather the total sum of money potentially in play where you are, for as long as you happen to be there. In today's frenzy of NLHE popularity, I guarantee that that sum is greater than your theoretical earn for any session you play, no matter how long or how well.

Another sign of a good game is a high joviality factor. If people are laughing and chatting, they may not be playing their best, most focused game; indeed, they may not even be interested in that, but rather in having a good social experience of poker. If, on the other hand, everyone is locked in stony silence, with their concentration turned up high, you're not likely to crack that game open like an egg. It's never good for us when our foes are playing well, or even making their best effort to do so.

You also want to note how many players are seeing the flop, and how many are limping versus raising. A game with lots of limpers and few raisers is a game you can beat with a number of different strategies. A game with few limpers and aggressive raisers requires a much narrower, more disciplined, less creative approach. Ideally you'll find a game that plays to your strengths, one you can beat by playing as you play best.

Reflecting on your own long experience of watching and waiting for a seat to open, what other at-a-glance indicators do you use, or could you use, to know whether a game is good or not? How do you recognize if a given game plays to your strengths?

>>

One opportunity I'm always on the lookout for is the newly spread game, especially if it's a fixed min/max game. Of such games there is one thing I know for sure and one thing I strongly suspect. The thing I know for sure is that the game will start on a level playing field; everyone will have exactly the same amount of money, which means I won't have to fight uphill against many big stacks. The thing I suspect is that at least a few of the players sitting in will not yet be mentally prepared to play well. They might have just rolled in off the freeway, or they may have been waiting a long time for a seat and are now impatient. I may be wrong about this. It may be that all of my foes are perfectly centered and perfectly patient. If that's the case, so be it. I'm going to take my time, in any event, to *breathe in* to the game, and get a strong feel for the players and the play before I start making any big moves.

I borrow the phrase "breathing in" from *Dispatches,* Michael Herr's classic book of Vietnam, and adapt its meaning to poker thusly:

TO BREATHE IN TO A POKER GAME
IS TO TAKE YOUR TIME AND USE
YOUR POWERS OF OBSERVATION
TO GET TO KNOW YOUR FOES.

The ones you've never faced before you obviously need to solve, but even if you've played against them many times, you need to update your understanding about how they're playing today. Their approach will necessarily vary according to their mood and means, how they've been running, whether they're on tilt, and related factors. It's dangerous to assume that someone will play weak, loose poker today, just because that's how she's played before. For all your foes, your goal is to build a working hypothesis about their skill level, risk affinity, (un)predictability, creativity, and so on. Whether this is a matter of assigning individual labels (my preference) or just noting who's active in the game and who's not, that's up to you. Just plan on not playing a lot of hands to start. I can think of no more firm foundation for a successful poker session than a good, long stint of breathing in.

It's a foundation many players intend to build, yet few actually do, for as self-evident as the advice may be—"take your time getting to know the other players"—it flies in the face of chasing the buzz. Those players who *came to play* draw no distinction between the first hand of a session and the last. For them to go a long time without getting playable hands is hard enough—and some people consider two hands too long—but to willfully lay down playable hands early merely for the sake of patience and foundation and knowing their foes, well, that just seems *wrong*. Even players who set winning (as opposed to having fun) as their goal will play too many hands too soon, following the dubious logic that they can't start to win until they start getting involved.

To see the utility of not getting involved, consider this example concerning the play of little pairs out of position.

Say it's your third hand at the table and you pick up pocket fives under the gun. If you knew that everyone behind you would passively limp into the pot, you'd call, looking for correct odds to draw to your set. If you knew that everyone behind you would obligingly fold to a raise, you'd raise, content to steal the blinds. But since it's just your third hand at the table, you can't know any of this stuff for sure. Later on, deeper in the session, you'll have sufficient information about your foes to know whether, and how, to play those pocket fives. In the meantime, why not just *fold and watch* here? Your attentiveness will be rewarded with *something*—some information about how one or another of your opponents plays one or another of his hands. Fold. Fold and wait. Breathe in.

Does this mean that you should throw away pocket aces? Of course not. Clearly playable hands are clearly playable, no matter what. To fold pocket aces just because you don't know your foes would be unjustified timidity. Granted, you don't know them, but also they don't know you—and they don't know you have pocket rockets right now. But for those marginal starting hands that you *could* or *could not* play—your K-Q suited, your A-T offsuit, your damn LPOPs (little pairs out of position)—why not err on the side of tightness while you're yet breathing in? Recalling that being inconsistent and unpredictable means choosing from among correct alternatives, the hand you play conservatively now, when information is shallow and scarce, is one you can play aggressively later, when information is plentiful and deep.

Apart from practicing patience and taking the time to know your foes, can you think of any other reasons to go slow at the start of a session?

>>

I can think of several. For one thing, remember that while you're trying to figure out your foes, they're trying to figure you out, too. To play uncharacteristically snug is to give them a misleading line on your play. As we discussed earlier, in the manner of establishing your fastball, your steal attempts will be more successful if you play them off a tight image. Folding most hands to start a session, then, both gives you the leisure to suss out your foes and gives them a chance to build a false impression about you.

In the newly spread game, it also gives someone, or several someones, the chance to go on tilt. This is simple human (poker) nature: Put nine or ten players around a poker table for even an hour, and the wheels are bound to come off *somebody's* bus. Calm, cool, and collected you, meanwhile, are just sitting there watching and noting, so that when you're finally ready to go on the attack, you know who your choice victims are.

Additionally, going slow will keep you from making a big, early mistake—the kind of mistake that gets your session off on the wrong, possibly catastrophically wrong, foot. Now look, I know you can wake up with pocket aces on your first hand and lose your whole stack to a lucky underdog. That happens. But why put yourself in an early pickle through a lot of early ill-considered, underinformed reckless adventures?

Think about the poker sessions you've played where you've dug yourself into an early deep hole. While you may have been able to dig yourself out again, and even racked up a nice win in the end, wouldn't it have been better *not to dig the hole at all?* Yes, yes, I know: Life is one long poker game and the re-sults of individual sessions shouldn't matter. Nor would they matter if we had perfect discipline and perfect awareness. But for those who fall short of perfection (all of us, yeah?) losing *irks* us. If we lose early and get irked, we run the risk of playing irked for the rest of the session, which is likely not to be prof-itable and certainly will not be fun.

Let me tell you something I know about myself: If my session gets off on the wrong foot, it's likely to suck for a long, costly time. If this is a problem you don't have, I stand in awe of your tranquility. But if it's a problem you *sometimes* have, or a problem you might have and don't know it or won't admit it, I want you to do something silly for me. Photocopy the following fortune cookie slogan—here, I'll put it in a nice iconic typeface for you—

> *NOT PLAYING* WELL
> BEATS *NOT PLAYING WELL*

—and cut it out and laminate it in plastic. Take it with you next time you play. Put it where you can see it. It might inspire you to the discipline you need to get your session off to a thoughtful, patient start.

Again, I want to stress that many foes you face will find this level of extreme patience anathema. They'll find it daunting in you because they'd find it impossible for themselves. They just can't stand the thought of surrendering lots of blinds and thereby losing money without giving themselves at least a *chance* to win some back. Pros or would-be pros will argue that not playing hands is simply too costly a strategy, a drain on their hourly win rate. Especially if there's a seat fee to be paid, they'll fret, how can they afford to *just sit there?* Why, they'd be better off not even being in the game; if they're not going to play hands, why don't they just get up from the table and stand there and watch?

You know what? Why don't they? Certainly they could learn as much about the other players by sweating the game as by occupying a seat and not playing hands. All they'd miss out on is the opportunity to establish their own tight image, though as we'll see in the next chapter, establishing that tight image is key to an overall session plan.

But let's be honest. All this talk about seat rental fees and surrendering blinds and negative impact on win rate is really just a rationalization, an excuse to chase buzz, and the sooner we admit that the buzz is part of what brings us to the table, the better off we'll be. You could look at the strategy of breathing in as a matter of delayed gratification: Deny the buzz now and reap the benefits later. You could also consider that your hourly win rate is amortized over all the hours you play, and that the mistakes you avoid early in sessions will certainly contribute to the plus side of your ledger. Really, though, I think it comes down to deciding that breathing in is a strategy you want to adopt (or not, you know—you always have that choice) and that to implement the strategy effectively, you have to do nothing for a long period of time.

How long does it take to breathe in to a poker game? My rule of thumb is three laps around a ten-handed table. In the realworld, this will take upward of an hour, which will seem like forever. Online, the same 30 hands might take only ten minutes—which will seem like double forever. In either realm, it will certainly be a challenge to your patience. Remember, though, that you're not *doing nothing* during this time. You're studying your foes closely, which should take all your attention and help you beguile the time. You're also giving the rest of the table strong reason to believe that you're a nonentity in the game. You might say that breathing in isn't really finished until everyone has completely forgotten you're there.

And what do you do if you pick up a playable hand during this time? Why, play it, of course. This business of breathing in should be a strategy, not a fetish. Just remember to narrow your definition of "playable hand" during this phase. Use Sklansky's Group 1 holdings—A-A, K-K, Q-Q, J-J, A-K—as your guide, and don't stray far from this path. You'll get these hands sufficiently infrequently that playing them will not destroy your preternaturally tight image. However, and I want to stress this, there's no harm in not playing *any* hand. Remember that you're flying blind here: You don't know your foes. Even a big hand can trap you if you're unwary, and based on what you know so far, you don't know whom to be wary of yet.

If you're presented with unraised big blinds, go ahead and accept what Layne Flack calls "infinite implied odds." But don't feel like you have to defend your blind against raises. You don't, not at this stage. In fact, you want to create the specific impression that you *don't* defend your blinds, so that when you do defend later (among your other activist strategies) they'll think you have a real hand. Nor should you be eager to complete the small blind, even if you think you're getting correct odds to do so. There are two reasons for this. First, completing the small blind is the hallmark of a loose (okay, possibly correctly loose) player, and that's not the image you're trying to sell here. Second, you're out of position against a whole lot of players you don't yet know. While you might flop huge and win a pot, it's more likely that you'll flop somewhat less than huge and get yourself involved in the very sort of costly adventure that the breathing in strategy is designed to prevent.

Your postflop play should be similarly circumspect. If you walk into a monster, sure, play it like a monster. But tread lightly when you have doubts. Suppose you've picked up pocket kings in late position, raised, and gotten one caller. Now there's an ace on the flop and it's checked to you. Should you bet? If you don't, you'll look like a wimp—*but there's nothing wrong with looking like a wimp right now!* Especially since you don't yet know enough about your foe to know whether he'd trap with a good ace, call with a bad one, or pay you off with a worse hand like pocket tens. Yes, you might have the best hand, and yes, you might get paid. Or you might get hammered. Either way, you're contemplating a high variance move—you'll go way up or way down—and high variance is not what you want right now.

This business of breathing in may seem to you to be unrealistically passive poker, tight to the point of asphyxia. However, since it does require a degree of restraint that many no limit players can't manage, it will definitely fill you with a feeling of superiority when you pull it off. Not only that, it will cause a sea change in the way you think about poker. Where most players go looking for a reason to get involved, you'll now go looking for a reason *not* to get involved. When every fold represents the triumph of meeting the goal you've set for yourself, you'll suddenly find that discipline comes easy. More than that, discipline isn't even discipline anymore. It's just the way you play the game. To see this phenomenon in the clearest light, consider the difference between *frustration* and *volition*. When you fold out of frustration, to fold is hell. But when you fold out of volition, to fold is bliss, pure bliss.

And it sets the stage for the fireworks to come. The fireworks of the big fat middle.

8

THE BIG FAT MIDDLE

♧ ♤ ◇ ♡

With breathing in as part of your strategic attack, having adequate playing time becomes even more critical to your success. Once you've taken the time to lay the groundwork for your winning session, you now need sufficient time to reap the reward. Were you to try breathing in to a short session, your efforts to decipher your foes would be wasted, for no sooner would you have adequate knowledge about them than it would be time to go, and you'd be walking that knowledge right out the door. Think of breathing in, then, as your planting season, and the rest of your session as your harvest. Use this thinking to keep from rationalizing hit-and-run sessions that you don't have enough time to prepare for properly or exploit profitably.

While you're in the game, and after you're done breathing in, you're in the phase I call *the big fat middle*. Here is where your early attentiveness will start to pay off, though of course you won't cease being attentive. Having gotten a firm line on the other players at the table—whom to attack and whom to avoid—you're now ready to open up your game a little. You'll do so with confidence for, beyond the clear sense of your enemies you now possess, your image is ripe for a move into high gear.

Let's muse upon this for a second, because people always

talk about the benefit of changing gears in poker, and while the underlying assumption is that changing gears from fast to slow and from slow to fast are equally good, this is not necessarily so. Just think about the times you've made the conscious decision to slow down at the poker table. What has motivated that switch? Usually it's a reversal of fortune. Maybe you've been caught speeding, and so now know that you can't bluff for a while. Perhaps you've taken a big stack hit and suddenly don't feel so frisky or so strong. Often it happens that we find our power moves trumped by someone even more aggressive than we are, and against such a player we have no choice but to dial it back and wait for better times. Granted, there are times when you'll back off just for the sake of mixing up your play, but in the main, when it comes to switching gears,

THE SHIFT FROM FAST TO SLOW
IS USUALLY A *DEFENSIVE SHIFT*.

Now let's look at a move in the other direction. You've been laying back, playing tight, not really being any sort of force at the table. Then something changes. Maybe it's the table composition, with strong players leaving and Timmies taking their place, tipping the balance of aggression in your favor. Or it could be that a run of good cards creates the impression that you're on a rush, yielding profitable opportunities for feisty play. Maybe it's the simple awareness that *now's the time to hit the gas,* a conscious decision consciously arrived at and coolly executed. In all events,

THE SHIFT FROM SLOW TO FAST
IS USUALLY AN *OFFENSIVE SHIFT*.

The shift from slow to fast after breathing in is particularly effective because it takes your enemies by surprise. Remember

that from their point of view you've been a nonentity, virtually an empty seat at the table. Now, suddenly, you wake up
and start getting all involved. At first your foes will assume
that you're a typical tightie who's been waiting for good cards
and has finally found some. This will be good for some blind
steals and some orphan adoptions. Soon it will occur to your
foes that you're playing too many hands for it just to be a sudden run of good cards. Now they're confused. You're not the
player they thought you were at all. They'll form various hy-
potheses, the most likely being that you'd tried to stay tight,
but your discipline finally broke and now you're playing fast
and loose just like everybody else. They'll think you're like
that vulture in the cartoon, the one that looks down from its
perch and says, "Patience my ass, I'm gonna *kill* something."

Let them think what they think. They're playing poker.
You're playing the big fat middle.

There are two ways to make this move into the BFM: arbi-
trarily or organically. As with the Crazy Ivan raising strategy,
you might just tell yourself, "At the top of the hour, the gov-
ernor comes off the engine." Alternatively, you can let the cards
dictate your speed by adding lower pocket pairs, unpaired paint,
and medium suited aces into your mix of playable hands. I like
to make my first move into the BFM with one of my package
hands like middle suited connectors. Poker is about winning,
of course, and not about gloating, but I have to admit that I
take delight in flabbergasting my foes when, after having done
nothing since I sat down, I now show down 7-8 suited for my
first winner. They just can't fathom how *that* was the first hand
I decided to like. Waiting patiently for big pocket pairs . . .
that's something they understand. But waiting for middle
suited connectors?

From their paradigm it makes no sense. But ours is a different paradigm. Among other things, we know all of our foes
better than they know us, because we've seen them in action
and they've seen nothing of our strategy and tactics. Presumably,
if you're in there raising with 7-8 suited, it's because you ex-

pect your intended target to pay you off with A-J or A-Q when the board comes 8-little-little. If you don't have that expectation, you don't attack that target. More important, you're playing the game from a global perspective, while most of your foes are stubbornly stuck in local mode, playing from hand to hand, hoping to pick up good cards, and hoping to get paid off.

Many years and many books ago, in the original *Killer Poker,* I wrote about a little game-within-the-game called *Raise!*

> *Imagine that you're playing poker, but imagine that you're also playing a secret game called "Raise!" where the object of the game is to raise as much as possible—the more raises you make, the higher your score. To your enemies, your actions would look reckless, a mistake, but according to your hidden rules, you're playing exactly correctly—a winning strategy in a completely different game.*

That's what we're going for here: a winning strategy in a completely different game. In service of that strategy, here's another concept I'd like you to contemplate:

IN NO LIMIT HOLD'EM, SMALL POTS DON'T MATTER.

This idea may strike you as counterintuitive. That's okay. It strikes a lot of sensible people as counterintuitive, which is why it's such a powerful tool for those who adopt it. The unwillingness to surrender small pots (and resulting over-defense of blinds and loose calls with middling hands) is a holdover in many people's minds from their experience in limit hold'em, where a good player figures to earn one to one and a half big bets per hour, and a couple of small pots won or lost can make or break that hourly win rate. A good no limit hold'em player likewise likes to achieve an average hourly earn somewhere in the neighborhood of twice the big blind, but the mechanics of that earn are entirely different. Your hourly win rate (or loss rate) will eventually regress toward the mean, but in the meantime, you'll experience some massive spikes in profit or loss, spikes determined by the outcomes of your big confrontations, not your small ones.

To a large degree, it doesn't matter whether you play small pots or not. Really. Let's say you go three laps in a $1–$2 blind game without defending your blinds. That's nine bucks. Now a hand comes along where you pick up pocket queens, raise to $8 preflop, and get a call from the big blind, who then folds when you bet the flop. You've made your money back. Or let's say that you drive those pocket queens into pocket jacks and pick up someone's $100 stack. Your investment in the blinds is insignificant by comparison.

This is why we won't concern ourselves with small pots, even after we've loosened up our starting requirements in the BFM. When offered the opportunity to contest for a small pot, we'll do one of two things: either decline the invitation; or try to build it into a big one. Which tack we take will depend on how we feel about risk, how deep the money is around us, and how well or poorly that money is defended. Let me give you an example of a hand you'll either choose to play or not play depending on the foe you face.

In a $5–$10 blind game, with about a grand in front of you, you hold double infinity—pocket eights—in middle position. You limp in and it's folded around to the button, who raises to four times the size of the big blind. Her stack is about the same size as yours, so the potential is there for a big money clash. It's folded back around to you. Should you call, raise, or fold? Notice that you can't even begin to address this question without first considering what you know about your opponent. Notice also that, having taking sufficient time to breathe in, you now know plenty.

Let's say your foe is a tightie/Timmy. Evidence indicates that she never raises without a premium hand, even in steal position. Further, she won't make continuation bets unless she hits her hand. There's not much chance that you're ahead in the hand, since the only non-pair hands she'll bet are A-K or A-Q. If you are ahead, you're only slightly ahead, and if you're behind, you're *way* behind. Contemplating prospective flops, you realize that there's almost no flop you can bet. If the board comes little, you'll fear her overpair. If it comes big, you'll fear that she hit her paint. You'd need an eight, which you don't have odds to draw to, or a draw, which you *won't* have odds to draw to, or a ragged board like J-7-2. The latter sort of flop is the only one you can comfortably bet, for you will (or anyway should) be able to drive off a tight, unimaginative player who's only holding overcards. But what if she's not on overcards? What if she's on a big pair and reraises? Then you'll have to surrender the hand, and your investment. Better to let it go early because in this case you're only likely to build a decent pot if your foe is holding a better hand.

A lot of players have trouble letting go of this hand in this situation. Even after they've made the right read and put their opponent on an appropriate range of hands, they look back down at that double infinity and think, *Well, darn, it* is *a pocket pair, and who knows? I might flop a set and take her off her whole stack.* While there's much to be said for implied odds in NLHE, let's not get carried away with the concept. Yes, your implied odds are significant *if* things break your way. But they'll only break your way if you hit your set *and* she hits enough of the flop to be interested. And at that you might not be in command. Suppose the flop comes A-K-8. If she's on A-K you're ahead (though not a lock), but where are you if she's on A-A or K-K? Hard as it is to get away from your lovingly held pocket pair in the face of a preflop raise, it's that much harder to get away from a flopped set, as you well know.

Not for nothing, remember that you're not just trying to *force* big confrontations. You're also trying to, you know, *win* them.

Now let's look at this scenario again, only this time we'll

tag your foe as a cowboy, capable of making a real estate raise in late position with a wide range of hands and, critically, almost certain to make a continuation bet on the flop. Now when she raises to $40 preflop and it's folded around to you, you can be much more comfortable calling. Why?

>>

The way I see it, you base your call on two factors. First, you can reliably predict that she'll bet whether she hits or misses. Second, most of the time she'll miss. This gives you all sorts of flexibility with all sorts of flops. If the flop produces any kind of draw, for instance, you can check-call the flop, and then bet phantom outs on the turn. If the flop is ragged, you can check-raise it, representing confidence that you're in the lead. If the flop comes orphan, you can bet out in an attempt to adopt. Plus, of course, you might actually hit your set. All of these options are available to you because you know your foe and know that she might not have a hand. Thanks to her aggressiveness, there's a pot out there worth winning, and thanks to your conscientious work of reading her, you have a number of ways to win it.

Take a moment and see your image through your foe's eyes. If you're only now entering the BFM, your image will seem super tight. Here again we see the advantage to a leisurely breathing in: Since you've done so much of nothing up till now, any action you take—any action whatsoever—will seem suspicious and threatening to her.

If you've been in the BFM for a while, and have started to mix it up some, you have a different image card to play, one where your foe's picture of you *and of herself* will make her surrender the pot. After all, it's no secret to her that she's been playing fast and loose, and she figures that you must know this, too. Since loose play often inspires loose play, and since you've started to get more involved, she may believe you capable of calling with as wide a range of hands as she's capable of raising with. Let's say the board is J-T-x and you check-raise. If she's on A-9, she's going to have an easy time believing that you hit the flop, and a very hard time calling.

Must you make this move? Of course not. Since small pots don't matter, there's nothing wrong with surrendering pre-flop, even against a foe you know to be stealing. Let 'em steal! This will just embolden them to keep stealing, giving you better opportunities to trap, or bluff-trap, later. But notice the critical difference between the two examples we've just looked at. In the first instance, there's only one workable path through the hand: You hit, you win. In the second case, there's much more room to move, and several different success scenarios. Your cards are the same. The flops are the same. The only difference is your foe. That's why we say:

READS ARE EVERYTHING.

Reads become complex when there are several players in the hand, for each will have their own approach, and those approaches may or may not be compatible with your own plans. Sometimes the presence of many players in the pot creates a problem you simply can't solve. If you're first to act against one tight player and the board is 3-4-5, even if the flop missed you, you can go ahead and bet to capture the pot. Against four players, though, with images ranging from tight to loose to frisky to clueless, your bet can hardly hope to have the desired result of folding the field. Yes, you might get rid of the tight player, but some of the others will come along for the ride, bad news for you if you're in there with nothing.

But suppose you're in a hand against one very tight player and one very loose one. The flop is K-7-6, and you hold A-7. Now your foes' proclivities are complementary to each other, and to your plan for the hand. In this instance if you bet, you might very well drive the tight player off a draw, while getting the loose player to stick around with a worse seven or even a naked ace. Reads. Reads are everything.

I feel like I've led you astray in this last example, suggesting that you should definitely attack either the 5-4-3 flop or the K-7-6 flop. In both instances, the pot may be sufficiently small that you won't even bother because, as I've said, small pots don't matter. But if, as I've said, small pots don't matter, then *what does*? What sorts of hands should we look to get involved with and how, exploiting all the manifest advantages of the BFM, shall we go about winning them? The short answer is this:

IT'S ALL ABOUT THE STACKS.
EVERYTHING ELSE IS JUST A JOUST.

The long answer lies in the chapter ahead.

9

PLAYS OF THE BIG FAT MIDDLE

In this chapter we're going to look at some common confrontations of big bet poker, and see how the union of our reads, our image, our math skills, and our clarity of vision can give us a plan for the hand and, ultimately, do the job of moving large numbers of chips from our foes' stacks into our own. At various decision points along the way, we'll stop and "open the moment" so that you can think about what you would do in that spot. And while there are clearly some *wrong* answers (such as giving draws the proper odds to call), there are very few *purely right* answers. So don't get too hung up if your path through the hand doesn't match mine (maybe yours is better). The real point of the exercise is to familiarize yourself with recurring hold'em situations so that you can make excellent decisions based on, if you will, previously stockpiled analysis.

Do you remember that old summer camp game, capture the flag, the object of which was to steal your enemy's flag while simultaneously protecting your own? I'd like you to consider that no limit hold'em cash games are very much like capture the flag—substituting, of course, stacks for flags. Your goal in the game should be to try to capture other players' stacks while not relinquishing your own. This means, generally, forcing big confrontations when you have the best of it and declining them when you don't. Let's look at some examples now.

POCKET ACES VERSUS A FLUSH DRAW

Holding pocket aces, you're heads-up against a foe you're pretty sure is on a flush draw. The question here is how will you manipulate the betting so as to maximize your return if he misses his draw, yet minimize your loss if he hits? Let's start by winding the betting back to before the flop, so we know how you got here and how much money's in the pot. For the sake of conversation, we'll set the blinds at $2–$5, give you two black aces in middle position, and have you open an un-raised pot for $20—not a bad raise with pocket aces, since you want to thin the field and, according to your read of this game, a bet of four times the big blind will drive out the shoe clerks. In this case you got just one caller, a kosher player in the cutoff seat. You know him to be smart enough to calculate pot odds, but not necessarily disciplined enough to follow through on what the odds dictate.

Now here comes the flop: K♥-6♥-2♦. There's $47 in the pot (less rake). Will you bet; if so, how much?

>>

Here's a case where the onus of the continuation bet works in your favor, since you're expected to bet, and you really want to anyway, for three reasons that I can think of: 1) A bet can win the pot right here. 2) A bet can extract extra value. 3) A bet can reveal new information. For the sake of taking a shot at doing all three jobs, I generally like to bet about two-thirds the size of the pot here. If my foe missed the flop completely, he'll fold to any bet anyhow. If he hit some, but not much, of the flop, my bet may be small enough and seemingly timid enough to keep him in the pot. (Remembering that the continuation bet is expected here, many optimistic foes will put you on a naked or nearly naked bluff). And if he calls without raising, he reveals something important about his hand. In the case of the two-suited board, he may be revealing that he's on a flush draw. He shouldn't call here—"draws are death in no-limit"—but again, this is a foe we can count on to be aware of the right thing, but not necessarily able to do it. For the sake of the implied odds (the greedy bastard thinks he's going to capture our whole stack), it's possible he'll take a card off.

Have we given him the right price to do so? Let's do the math.

When he flops a flush draw, he's about a 1 in 3 shot to complete that hand by the river. Should the pot be offering him more than a 2–1 ROI, he's correct to call. With $47 in the pot, our roughly two-thirds bet of, say $35 will put $82 in the pot. Our opponent has to call $35 to win $82. Certainly that's better than 2–1—but only if he gets to see the river for free. He can't figure us not to bet again if the turn is a blank (for if we put him on a flush draw, not betting again would be a huge mistake, and we try not to make those). If he's planning or willing to fold to a bet if he misses on the turn, then he really needs about a 4–1 ROI on flop action because he's about 4–1 against catching on the next card alone. Since he doesn't currently have sufficient ROI, he should fold.

But many players aren't that smart or that disciplined. They routinely confuse the overall odds of making a hand with the odds of completing on the next card—sometimes willfully deluding themselves—and make their calling decisions accordingly. Occasionally, you'd like to spell it out for them: *You don't have odds to call here, shoe clerk! Fold!* That's a signal you can send by slightly overbetting the pot on the flop. Bet more than the size of the pot—about one-third more—and you'll make it abundantly clear that it will cost your foe plenty, and plenty again on the turn, to see the river with you this hand.

What we're contemplating, then, is a range of possible flop bets, from somewhat less to somewhat more than the size of the pot. The exact size of your wager should be based on your goal, your disposition, and your read. Would you rather not gamble? Then bet more and drive him off the pot. Will he call a smaller bet here and call again if he blanks the turn? Then bet the low end of the spectrum. Don't forget to take stack size into account, for while you may be making a prohibitively large wager, your foe might have only enough chips left to make an odds-friendly call. All of these considerations taken together amount to *tuning your bet,* scaling it to fit the circumstance. Before you go throwing "standard" bets and raises into the pot, always pause to ask yourself what amount amounts to the right tool for the right job.

One thing you definitely don't want to do is price your opponent into this pot with a hoover bet. Suppose instead of betting $35 on the flop, you bet only $10. *He'll have to call that,* you chortle, *more money for me.* Yes, he'll have to call. You're giving him a better than 5–1 return on a 4–1 shot for just the turn card alone. To give a foe favorable calling odds here is a fundamental math mistake—one usually motivated by greed and the misguided desire to milk a few extra chips. Don't fall into this trap.

Of course, you could always check the flop, check the turn, check the river, and hope your aces hold up, but that's an extreme example of risk averse play, and if you're *that* risk averse you probably don't belong in the game in the first place. NLHE rewards aggression. You must be in the practice of betting and raising when you think you have the best of it—or can get the best of it by betting and raising. In this case, you can tune your bet according to your plan for the hand, but in all events, try to bet big enough to encourage the drawing hand to make the right move by laying down, or a big mistake by calling.

But the best laid plans, as they say. Suppose you tune your bet to the plus side of pot size and still get called. And further suppose that the turn card is a third heart. Now you're out of position against a foe you've put on a draw—and the draw you put him on just got there. What would you like to do now, apart from rolling back time 15 seconds and putting a blank on the board instead?

>>

Here's where you really have to lean on your reads and your tags. As already stipulated, you've observed this foe long enough to know that he'll take a draw when the odds don't warrant. Now a new question emerges: Will he bet phantom outs? Is he tricky enough to call on the flop and bet at a scare card on the turn? If you know him to be *glatt* kosher (fully and completely straightforward), you can check or bet small, and get away from the hand if you face severe heat. If he's got some frisky in him, though, you're in a pickle, because you run the twin risks of betting into a made hand or letting a bluff drive you out. Looking back, this is exactly why you overbet the flop, for the express purpose of protecting your aces against a (real or perceived) killer card on the turn. But it didn't work out, oh well.

If you check here, it's possible that your kosher foe will check behind you. In that case, you can provisionally assume that he's on a pair lower than yours and not the flush draw at all. But only *provisionally* assume this, for as we've already discussed, players of a certain stripe (especially risk averse ones) are more likely to trap than to bluff. While your foe in this instance may not be tricky enough to bet phantom outs, he may very well be tricky enough to check his made hand.

If you don't figure your foe to be that supremely straightforward, it may be that the only way for you to win this pot is to bet at it again. If you check, you'll embolden him to bluff; however, if you bet *and* he's on phantom outs, he may put *you* on the made hand and decide to get out of your way. Or you could check, inviting the bluff, and then raise him back to drive him off the hand. This is a move that requires both boldness and a clear sense of your foe. You have to be pretty much dead sure that he didn't hit his hand or you're going to go off for a lot of chips. I don't need to tell you that betting into the best hand is a must to avoid.

If your primary sources of information (your tags and your reads) fail you, don't forget to prospect your secondary sources as well. Is he giving off tells in the moment? Can you broadcast some tells of your own to influence the action? How deep is his stack? Does he have enough to make a meaningful bet? Does he have the guts to bluff with his case chips? Is he the sort of player who's content to check down a hand?

What other secondary information could you source right here?

>>

Wheels within wheels, right? He *might* be on a draw and he *might* be on a bluff and he *might* be tricky and he *might* be kosher. If you check, you embolden him to bluff, but if you bet, you might face a raise—but if you don't bet, you're giving another free card . . . but if you do bet, you're betting into the best hand but but but but but . . . that way lies madness.

Just now I'm reminded of what a golf pro told me shortly before we both realized I had no aptitude for the sport and I gave it up completely. "You can't think about individual parts of your swing," he said. "You have to think about the swing as a whole. And then," he added, "not think about that, too." Golf is a very Zen sport. But poker's the same way. If we try to think about all these bits of information separately, we just whip up clouds of confusion. Somehow—and it's more of an art than a science—we just have to let all available information wash over us and wait for a coherent picture to emerge.

Above all, we have to *trust our reads*. There's simply no point in putting a foe on a hand or a plan or proclivity if we can't or won't follow through on what we've decided we see. Pocket aces are particularly troubling in this regard because our appraisal of the situation is often warped by that familiar sense of entitlement aces bring with them. After all, we had *aces*. They ran into trouble. The only way they can *not* be in trouble now is if our foe is bluffing. Therefore, we may delude ourselves into seeing bluffs that aren't there.

Make your decisions dispassionately. Don't compound your woes by stubbornly ascribing moral authority to your big pocket pair. If you're beat, you're beat. Move on.

BETTING OUT OF TROUBLE

"The best offense," it has been said, "is often a good pretense." Here's an example of how, having bet yourself into trouble, you can sometimes bet yourself right back out.

In a $200 buy in game with $3 and $5 blinds, you have about $250 in front of you. Your table image is that of a no-nonsense player who rarely gets out of line. On the hand in question you're dealt A♠-Q♠ on the button. A canny, frisky (but loose) player limps in from under the gun, and the cutoff makes it $15 to go. You know the cutoff to be someone you can outplay on the flop, especially in position, so you make it $55 to go, looking to get heads up against her.

Unfortunately, you don't happen to have noticed that the big blind has just $50 left. If you had noticed, you might have refrained from raising, for this is an extremely loose player, currently tilty, and currently looking for any excuse to felt himself and move on to his next rebuy. He calls all in, which inspires both the under the gun player and the cutoff to call as well. You wanted one caller, but now have three: two players with stacks comparable to yours and one who is all in, and thus bluffproof. It looks like rocky shoals ahead. What sort of holdings do you figure you're up against here, and how do you rate your chances of currently being ahead in the hand?

>>

The hand you fear worst, the one that dominates you most, is A-K. You don't figure either UTG or the cutoff for a premium pair; both are perfectly capable of reraising all in preflop. It's possible that the all-in player has aces or kings, but he has screaming tells; if he had a huge hand, his body would have betrayed him. The situation, then, is not entirely grim. You might be up against worse aces or lower pocket pairs. UTG might even have something like K-J or K-Q; he's just that frisky. Your big problem with UTG is that he's capable of making big bets on pure steals.

The flop comes K-3-3 rainbow. It's not a pure orphan, thanks to the one wheelhouse card, but it gives you some room to move. Of course you're not looking at the flop as it comes down; you've got your eyes glued to UTG, the most dangerous player in the hand. He doesn't look particularly happy, but doesn't seem to have given up on the hand entirely. He checks, though, as does the cutoff, and it's up to you. Now what?

>>

You could check behind them and hope either that your hand is the best or will improve. Or you could bet, hope they both fold, and take your chances against the all-in player. There's a good reason to bet here, and that's the diminished likelihood of a *curiosity call,* the call you get sometimes from players who should know better, but don't. Whether it's "calling for the size of the pot" or "calling to keep you honest," these calls can do evil things to your bluffs; however, with an all-in player in the pot, everyone's curiosity about your holding will be satisfied whether they call or not. Further, most players look askance at anyone who starts building side pots willy-nilly. You must have something, they reckon, or you'd be content to contend for the main pot alone. For these reasons, many players will fold without much thought in this situation and let the all-in player be their stalking horse. They're looking forward to seeing what a good laydown they made.

That's what you're counting on here when you bet just $50. Yes, that's a small bet for the size of the pot, but there are no draws out there, so you're not worried about giving anyone correct odds to call, and since your bet opens a side pot, it actually looks stronger than it is. They'll think you're hoovering, and since they'll get to see your hand no matter what, they won't give you the satisfaction of calling along. Note the underlying principle here:

USE THE PRESENCE OF AN ALL-IN PLAYER
TO LEVERAGE THE STRENGTH OF YOUR BET.

Note also that there's not much to fear in your foes' holdings. Threes and bad kings are unlikely—they wouldn't have called your preflop raise. Good kings are a threat, but many other hands that might have called you preflop—notably medium aces and a whole range of pocket pairs—will have real trouble calling you here. If your bet works, it will clear out the live players and leave you heads up against the all-in player, who could be in there with anything or nothing at all.

In this case it does work. Both active players fold (pocket sixes and pocket sevens, as it happens). The turn and the river are both blanks, and your A-Q holds up against the all-in player's A-8.

Were you lucky to beat the all-in player? Maybe. Tilty as he is, he could have called just as easily with K-Q (or K-3!) as with A-8. So call it a coin flip. But recognize that a coin flip was exactly what you wanted here. The goal of your bet was to drive out two players who A) might outdraw you; B) might already be ahead; and C) have enough chips left to put you to a hard choice. Or put it this way: You might be ahead against one of these players; you're not likely to be leading all three. The only way to win the hand, then (short of checking it down and getting lucky), is to drive your live opponents into the muck. Getting better holdings to fold is the goal, and the major accomplishment of your play in this hand.

Five important points to consider:

1. Make your plan for the hand. Know what you're going to do and why you're going to do it. Preflop, you cooked up the reasonable scheme of reraising a weak player in order to take the pot away after the flop.
2. Adjust your plan as necessary. When two others called, you had to alter your plan for the hand. Your first impulse may be to shut it down, check it down, and surrender the pot, but further thought, based on your knowledge of the other players and your sense of how they view you, could yield a better result.
3. Make the latest possible decision based on the best available information. Be clear-eyed and frank in your appraisal. When you get outcomes you didn't expect (such as more callers than desired), simply fit new facts into a new paradigm. "Always make room for the new idea," and make sure that your thinking isn't clouded by resentment or wishful thinking. Also be sure to include in your analysis such special circumstances as the presence of an all-in player and the diminished likelihood of a curiosity call.
4. Pick your fights. Make sure that the situation is exactly right for the moves you have in mind. You have a lot less to lose by cowering out than by forcing a confrontation you can't win, especially if it's one you *know* (but maybe won't admit) you can't win. That said . . .
5. Be bold. When you bet yourself into trouble, sometimes the only way to escape is to bet yourself back out. Fortune favors the bold. You needn't be reckless or careless, but don't fear to bet when betting is called for.

In all events, make it your practice to analyze the situation as the situation unfolds. Find a path through the hand, then follow that path. Guile and resourcefulness can earn you chips that cards alone would never send to your stack.

BUTTON, BUTTON, WHO NEEDS THE BUTTON?

The theme of this scenario is *the second liar never has a chance,* and it subverts the conventional wisdom that position is precious in NLHE. Hey, don't get me wrong: I like position as much as the next guy. It's just that there are times when being *first* to act actually puts you in a stronger position—times, in fact, when early position positions you to steal pots you otherwise couldn't capture.

Consider this example: In a $100 buy in game with $1 and $2 blinds, you find yourself in the big blind holding . . . well, for this play it really doesn't matter what you hold. We'll give you the hammer, 2-7 offsuit, just to demonstrate that sometimes the cards you hold matter as little as the position you're in.

It's folded around to the button. You'd expect him to make the standard real estate raise, wouldn't you? And he does. Why not? He's only got to get through the small blind and you, and you're both on random hands. If he has something even as middling as K-Q offsuit, he's almost a 2–1 favorite to have the best hand. He won't mind if you both fold, but he won't mind if you call, either, figuring to use the towering strength of precious position to take the pot away from you on most flops. Let's see if we can undo his strategy.

For this play, we want the small blind to fold, and she obligingly does. Now it's up to you. What would you like to do?

>>

I want to stress that there's absolutely nothing wrong with folding here. You'll never ever lose money by not playing this junk hand. And small pots don't matter. But there is one larger issue at stake, and that's how the button is treating your blinds. If you plan to stay in this game for a while, you'd like the button to leave your blinds alone, and this scenario may achieve that goal. Also contemplate where you are in relation to the big fat middle. If you've just come out of breathing in, this move has additional strength and a greater chance of success.

One possible course of action is to reraise, re-stealing on a naked bluff. But then you'll be expected to make a continuation bet on the flop, and that could put you in a bind if the flop comes unfavorable to your hand. Since most flops will come unfavorable to most hands (and almost every flop comes unfavorable to the hammer) you want to manipulate the situation so that the *unfavorable flop actually works in your favor.* So just call. Remember, the button puts you on a random hand. In other words, he has no clue what you hold. But you have at least some clue about what he has. By prior observation, you know exactly how much of a hand he needs to make a button raise. Obviously if you put him on a real hand, you fold, but if he's like most real estate raisers, he could be in there with any half-hand like K-T or 4-4 or even some real egregious cheese like 6-9 suited. Probably he's somewhat coordinated, because he'd like to have a little something-something to go to war with on the flop. Let's put him on any two cards higher than an eight.

To understand what happens next, remember the key fact that every unpaired hand misses the flop two-thirds of the time. And if the flop comes rich in low cards it's even more unlikely to have hit the real estate raiser's hand. Of course, you're also a favorite to miss most flops, but the crucial difference is *you get first crack at this one!* Position, in other words, is reversed. By being first to act, you can be first to lay claim to the pot.

Certain flops will be more attractive to you than others. Coordinated flops, especially high coordinated flops, are not good candidates for this steal, for two reasons. First, with myriad draws and high cards, your foe is more likely to see something he likes out there. Second, if that flop had actually hit your hand, wouldn't you be more likely to use the "weakness" of your position to trap by check-calling or check-raising? That's how your foe will read it, and he'll be chary of your bet into a coordinated flop.

A really ragged flop, though, can be your best friend because of the supposedly random hand with which you called preflop. Again, attend to your image. Are you *really* perceived as loose enough to call with cheese? Perhaps you're perceived as tight enough to call only with a big pocket pair. In all events, take a moment to see yourself through your foe's eyes. It's crucial that he sees you the way you want him to see you.

If he does, go ahead and bet. Bet like you own the flop. Make the same size bet you'd make if you had hit your hand. Your workhorse two-thirds pot bet is probably a good place to start; you can scale your bet from there depending on the prevailing betting practices at the table and upon what you know your foe knows about your own betting patterns. You do need to bet large enough so that it doesn't look like you're on a weak steal attempt (let's call this a *strong* steal attempt) and so you don't give adequate odds to draws. But go ahead and bet. Have the courage of your conviction. There's no point in getting involved in this pot in the first place if you're just going to cower out on the flop.

Could you check-raise bluff here? Sure, why not? If your foe is a fan of the ol' continuation bet, he may be obliged to whack at any flop. You check, he bets, you raise, he folds, next case. But I prefer to bet out for several reasons. First, you minimize your chip risk, getting the most bluff-bang for your buck. Second, if you check and he checks behind you, you've given him a free card. Third, if it's check-check and you then bet the turn, he can more reliably read your bet as a bluff. Fourth, most important, your goal here is secondarily to win the money in the pot, but primarily to send a signal resonating through the rest of the BFM. You want your foe to know that you're the sort of player who's not afraid to call out of position and then to come out betting. You want him to get the idea that attacking your blind is not in his best interest, and an aggressive lead bet into a ragged flop is likely to establish you in his mind as feisty and unpredictable. Next time he's got the button, he may decide not to tangle with you, which leaves you unmolested in the big blind, and what's not to love about that?

CROSSING THAT RIVER WHEN WE COME TO IT

I'm not a big fan of calling. I don't know any decently aggressive poker player who is. It's so much better to be the one driving the action, not just because it's generally good for your fierce 'n' fearsome image, but also because, of course,

YOU NEVER HAVE TO GET LUCKY
IF EVERYONE FOLDS.

Much as I hate calling in general, I *really* hate it on the river, where the only way I can win is to have the best hand. Since I might not know for sure whether I have the best hand, the river bet by its very nature puts me to a hard choice. This is another instance where the power of position is actually reversed. If my foe is stalwart enough to be the first one into the pot at the river, she has a good chance of putting my marginally callworthy hand to a difficult test.

The river situation is especially dicey when the pot has grown to a meaningful size. At that point, a river bet presents players with the unpleasant alternatives of either surrendering a sizeable pot or investing heavily in it when they might be beaten. Since you'd much rather be forcing this choice on others than facing it yourself, you generally want to be the one putting in that big bet on the river. This late stage aggressiveness has the further benefit of warning your foes off other pots later. Once they know that you'll club them with big river bets, they'll be reluctant to put themselves in a situation where such clubbing can take place.

But a river bet usually has to be a big bet. If it's not, it won't be taken seriously—nor should it. Betting $10 into a $200 pot is just ridiculous. Your foe would only have to catch you bluffing better than one time out of 20 in order to make calling profitable. So you bet big to demonstrate the seriousness of your intent. But what if they have a hand?

The argument against promiscuous river betting goes like this: "The only hand that can call you can beat you." Certainly there are times when this is true, and in such cases you should dial back your aggression. Say you've put your foe on a straight draw, and the card you think he's looking for gets there on the river. If you're certain he's made his hand there's not much point in betting, for he will certainly call or raise. Trouble is, if you *don't* bet and he *hasn't* made his hand, he may be emboldened to bluff, once again putting you to the hard choice of calling a big bet on the river.

What a mess, huh? Damned if you do, damned if you don't. Is there no way out of this thicket? Let's paint a picture and see.

You start the hand in late position with A-8 and face a raise from a middle position bettor. Since you know this player to be capable of raising with all premium hands and some sub-premium holdings like K-J offsuit or Q-J suited, you decide to see the flop. It comes A-9-7. Your foe bets two-thirds of the pot. What do you do, and why?

>>

The only holdings I fear here are good aces, and this player could be on many other hands, such as big pocket pairs, medium pocket pairs, or the aforementioned K-J or Q-J. My plan for the hand, then, is to call the flop and see where I stand on the turn. Ideally I'll hit my kicker; absent that, any low card may present me with an opportunity to take the pot away if it turns out that my foe isn't on a good ace and has no stomach for a fight. In this instance, a deuce comes off on the turn. She checks. I bet, expecting her to lay down her hand here. Surprisingly, she calls. Why would she do that?

>>

My first thought is that either she's trapping with a great ace or she thinks I'm trying to steal the pot. My second thought is that that's a weird little call. Something just doesn't smell right. Before I have a chance to form my third thought, the river card comes down. It's another deuce—and she makes a pot-size bet. This bet is troublesome for me, for it fits either possibility I contemplated on the turn: She could be on a good ace; she could be on a resteal. Since she had first crack and has come out betting, I have no choice but to make the hard choice. I don't want to call a better hand. I don't want to sur-render to a worse one. What should I do?

>>

I need to put her on a hand that's not only consistent with a river bet, but also consistent with her action on prior streets. Quickly reviewing the action up till now, I note that she raised preflop in middle position, which suggests some strength. Then she bet on the flop, which could be strength or just obligation. Then came that odd check-call on the turn, and that's the part that daunts me. I could understand a check-raise on the turn—that's how a good ace milks maximum return. But to just call . . . she can't expect me to bet again on the river if I'm not sure I have the best hand, nor can she expect me to call on the river if she bets for value. So it seems like the check-call on the turn sets up a lead bluff on the river. So she's stealing, right? I should call.

But my gut (and by gut, of course, I mean my history of examination) tells me that this player is not capable of that move. That call on the turn was really a conflicted action, like she was striking a compromise between a fold and a raise. Like she was caught between *hoping* she had the best hand and *fearing* she was beat. So, no, I don't think she's stealing. I think she's half convinced she has a winner, and she's betting to maximize return if she's right.

But I still don't know if she's right or not, so I'll seek my next source of information. I'll look at myself through her eyes. I'm in the BFM of my session, and have opened up my play, which she knows. She can easily peg me as frisky, and rate me as capable of calling her preflop raise with any ol' junk, including hands that produce draws. But she also knows, if she's paying attention, that I wouldn't call without proper drawing odds on the flop nor, certainly, decline the offer of a free card on the turn. So, despite how frisky she knows me to be, she can't put me on a failed draw here. Note that if my image were pure true value, it would be easy for me to get away from my hand here, for players generally don't bet into true value players on the river unless they're confident of holding the winner.

Is this a trap of my own making? Has my own perceived willingness to play anything or nothing at all given my foe the fuel to bluff? I still don't know.

Smarter players than I will take a pure math approach here, weighting the odds of her various possible hands—A-K, A-Q, K-K, K-J, etc.—and assigning the probability of her betting at the pot with a worse hand than mine. Next, they'll measure that probability against the ratio between bet size and pot size, and come up with a reasonable formula for making or not making the call. Know what? My math skills aren't that good. Nor are my thought processes that fast. Still, I feel certain that on most hands there's enough information out there to make a reasonable stab at my foe's holding, if I just allow myself to put the information together. What I'm looking for—and this will sound murkily metaphorical, I know, but it's true—is for all her possible hands to run through my mind like tumblers on a combination lock, until the hand I think she has eventually clicks into place.

I keep coming back to that check-call on the turn. If she thought she had me beat there, why didn't she raise? If she didn't think she had me beat, why did she call? Because she was on a legitimate draw? There's none out there, bar T-8 or 8-6, neither of which hands she would have raised with preflop. What else do I know? *What else do I know?!*

Suddenly it hits me. About an hour ago, when I was still breathing in, I saw her bet aggressively on the flop and the turn, only to check-call, and lose, when an ace fell on the river. I recall that she flashed pocket queens in disgust, and complained about always getting sucked out on.

Snap! She's got pocket queens, or maybe jacks or kings. Her check-call on the turn was, in fact, a compromise of conflict. She *wanted* her queens to be good, but *feared* that they were not. She probably knew she was beaten when I called on the flop, but that toxic combination of a big pocket pair and a sense of entitlement has gotten her stuck on the hand. When she checked on the turn, she no doubt hoped that I would check behind her and give her a free ride to the river. Well, that didn't happen, so then she went ahead and made a bad, loose call.

Comes the river, and she's lost in the hand. She knows she's beaten, doesn't *want* to be beaten, so convinces herself that I'm on the cheese end of my possible hands, the busted draw, even though she should have been able to conclude that I wouldn't take that draw. Or maybe she just figured that the only way to win the pot was to brazen it out. Tying all of these threads of consideration together, I decide that she's on a big pocket pair, and call. She turns over pocket jacks—okay, so I missed by one—and surrenders the pot.

Should I have reraised on the river? After all, if I'm so certain she's got a big pocket pair, why not try to extract a little extra value? I'll tell you why: Because I'm *certain,* but not *sure.* Even though my analysis led to a firm conclusion, my analysis could easily be wrong. While my foe is striking her compromise between conflicting emotions, I'm striking mine between risk and reward. If I'm right and I call, I'm going to win the pot. If I'm wrong and I call, I'm going to lose the pot. If I'm wrong and I reraise, I'm going to lose even more, or worse, be put to a decision for all my chips. After all, J-J is an iffy hand with an ace on the flop—but A-J and A-T are iffy hands there, too, and those are hands that can beat me.

Remember that NLHE is all about protecting your stack. Remember also that greed is a natural part of everyone's game, a component we must routinely police ourselves against. If I do get greedy here and reraise, I may be walking into one of those "the only hand that can call you can beat you" bear traps. It seems to me that the upside of a reraise here is small— she may throw more good money after bad—but the downside, unless I'm 100 percent sure of my read, could be catastrophic. Why not content myself with a decent pot?

Note that I might reraise all-in if I were holding something like T-T here and felt that a big reraise was the only way to win the pot.

Returning now to the question originally posed—"How do we get out of this mess?"—the answer seems to me both simple and dauntingly complex. We have to do a deep and thorough analysis of the hand when there's not enough time to do a deep and thorough analysis. We have to assign probabilities when probabilities are unassignable. We have to reach a conclusion based on available information when available information is both incomplete and subject to multiple interpretations. And we have to be willing to call and be wrong from time to time, lest we inspire our foes to bet us off every river we come to.

Ha! No one said the game was easy, right? But the more practiced we become at making these evaluations, the faster and more reliable our analyses become. We can't always be right, but we can always be getting better at thinking things through.

A BLUFF THAT SUITS YOUR STYLE

We'll close this chapter with a look at four varieties of the bluff. Remember that bluffing is a nuanced business. It's not just a matter of slugging away at the pot until everyone leaves. It's the confluence of cards, image, and circumstance, all glued together by both your real style and the style you're perceived to play. How, or even whether, you run a bluff may be controlled by as simple a thing as how long you've been playing, or what happened on the hand just prior. In any event bluffing is a necessary tool for big bet poker. If you only ever bet with the best of it, it won't take long for your savvy foes to get wise, and you'll never get action on your hands. Nor will you ever be able to bet yourself out of trouble, as in the example above.

Beyond that, the bluff is NLHE's most sublime move. When it works, you feel like Robin Hood, robbing from the rich and giving to, well, yourself. Pulling off a bluff gets you high, inspires you to stand up and do a little dance. Of course, bluffing shouldn't be about feeling, but rather about result: pots won or stolen that would otherwise have been surrendered or lost. Still, it's a fact that bluffing's a rush, so let's examine several ways to seize that buzz.

Name of Bluff: *The Unbearable Tightness of Being*

> YOUR IMAGE: You have a tight image. Your opponents have been trained by your infrequent calls and raises to believe that you know what a quality hand is (you do!) and that you never get involved without one (well . . . not *never*).

Your target: You want to run this bluff against an opponent who knows you to be tight, and who has gotten into the habit of driving you off second rate holdings with second rate holdings of his own.

The situation: Though you normally call or raise only with big pairs or big paint, look for a chance to flat-call a preflop raise from a known frisky opponent, no matter what you hold. Ideally you want a single foe, and you want position. Remember, she reads you as tight, so when you call behind her raise, she'll figure you for a reasonably high hand, something like A-J or K-Q suited.

The bluff: You'll need a favorable flop for this, one that contains at least an ace or a king, preferably both. Then, if your opponent checks, you bet. If she bets, you raise. She'll have no trouble folding; her knowledge that you're tight will easily lead her to conclude that the flop hit your hand.

Nuance: Adjust the size of your bet or raise to make it look like a hoover bet. In this circumstance, the small bet has the best chance of fitting your tight image and convincing your opponent you've hit your hand. As a bonus benefit, if she happens to have a real hand and hits you with a significant reraise, you can break off your bluff at minimal cost.

What next: Go back to sleep. Wait for your usual premium hand, or wait for enough hands to pass that your tight image has been reinforced and then go for another steal.

Caveat: This bluff is no good if you don't have the courage to run it. Once you call preflop, you are *not* looking to hit your hand. You're looking to hit a flop that *looks* like it hit your hand. Having set your opponent up for a bluff bet or raise, you have to pull the trigger. Otherwise, you're just wasting your chips.

Name of Bluff: *Loosey in the Sky (With Nothing)*

YOUR IMAGE: You have a loose image. If you're the sort of player who gets involved in a lot of hands, your opponents won't credit you with much of anything when you jump into the pot. That's okay; in this instance you'll use your perceived looseness against them.

YOUR TARGET: Aim this bluff at kosher, straightforward foes, true value players who know enough about poker to play the right kind of hands, but not necessarily enough to play all their hands right.

THE SITUATION: Having established the fact that you muck around with all sorts of strange holdings, set the hook by betting into, or accepting a raise from, a true value player. You know his hand: big pairs or big paint. He has the best of it going into the flop, but that doesn't matter because only a good flop will help his hand—but a wide variety of bad flops will help yours!

THE BLUFF: Like most flop-dependent bluffs, this one only works if the cards cooperate. If the flop comes all high cards, you're done with the hand because your foe won't credit you with having hit the flop, and you *know* that the flop helped him. But suppose the flop comes 8-7-6? You've trained your enemy to expect you to be in there with slop like 9-8 or 8-7, so when you bet out, how can he stick around? If all he has is a draw to overcards, he'll go running, and even if he has an overpair, he has to fear all those low straight cards that could knock him dead on the turn. Deciding that discretion is the better part of valor, he'll skedaddle, hoping to pound you with his big cards later.

NUANCE: Your best friend is the coordinated middle flop . . . but not *too* coordinated. You're better off, for example, betting into a two-flush than a three-flush on board, because the three-flush could embolden your foe to stick around with nothing but one suited overcard. Seek flops that don't help a good hand at all, but *could* help the kind of crap you're reputed to play.

WHAT NEXT: Keep on keeping on. If you can reliably put your foes on big hands but they can't reliably put you on anything, they're simply begging to give their money away. Just don't let them trap you; at the first sign of legitimate resistance, credit them with a real hand and get out of their way. Remember that your looseness frustrates them and they want to play back at you, but their tightness will prevent them from playing back unless they have a hand.

CAVEAT: Beware of a weak hit from a good hand. A flop like T-6-3 or J-7-8 could spell big trouble for your bluff attempt since your true value foes could easily have called you preflop with A-T suited or J-Q suited. Since they know you to be a lying sack of cheese, they're likely to call when you bet, and beat you with the best hand. You'd much prefer a flop so ragged that no sensible person could have a piece of it; hence, your reputation as "no sensible person" will allow you to bet and win.

Name of Bluff: *Slick Rick and The Orphan Flop*

YOUR IMAGE: You're in control of the game. For whatever reason—savvy bets, native intelligence, or chiseled good looks—you have become *Slick Rick*, the straw that stirs the drink. From this power position, you can lay claim to pots that others will willingly surrender.

YOUR TARGET: The fearful. Those against whom you've already had some success. Maybe you've shown down some winners against them. Maybe you've raised them off a pot or two. For whatever reason, they've made it clear that they don't want to go to war with you.

THE SITUATION: Having proven both a willingness to bet aggressively and an understanding of when and how to make your power moves, you've got most of the rest of the table looking to avoid trouble from you. Maybe it's just that you have a mountain of chips and no one wants to be crushed by it.

THE BLUFF: This bluff is simply a run at an orphan flop, and when you're running the table you should consider all orphan flops to be yours for the taking. Even if your opponents don't credit you with a real hand, they do credit you with a willingness to keep on betting, and for some that's pressure they won't want to face.

NUANCE: If your foes are hip to the idea that there's nothing wrong with surrendering small pots, they'll likely let their hands go even if they know you're stealing. Remember, though, that it's not impossible for someone to hit an orphan flop. (Or what serves as a hit—holding 8-8 to a flop of 7-3-3, for example.) If you encounter an opponent too willing to call, just shut down your betting. Don't bluff off your stack into a made hand.

WHAT NEXT: Keep your eye peeled for other such *flopportunities*. Especially in weak, timid, low buy in NLHE games, the pot often goes to the first player to lay claim.

CAVEAT: Wise players will get wise to your tricks. Should someone check-raise you over an orphan flop, it's best to surrender, take note of the player who made that quality move, and adjust your stealing strategy accordingly.

Name of Bluff: *Caught Stealing—And Stealing Again*

YOUR IMAGE: You've been caught bluffing in the recent past. Now that the flush of embarrassment has faded, you're turning your attention to the salient question of how to use your larcenous table image against your foes.

YOUR TARGET: Prideful, arrogant, ego-driven players who have recently enjoyed the satisfaction of catching you with your hand in the cookie jar. They wouldn't mind snapping you off again, because thieving bastards like you need to be kept in your place.

THE SITUATION: You were caught bluffing. It felt like the end of the world. It wasn't. It was the end of your old image— tight—and the start of your new image: stung by defeat, in psychic pain, and capable of almost any eccentricity.

THE BLUFF: Should you be fortunate enough to pick up a real hand shortly after having been caught stealing, you have the opportunity to essay what looks like a *tilt-driven drive.* Your opponents won't credit you with good cards. They'll assume that you're still smarting from your recent setback and, like so many of them would, are now trying to get well soon by pushing another hand too far, too fast. In this instance, you're actually bluffing that you *don't* have a hand . . . "bluffing with the best of it," in fact.

NUANCE: Your foes know you just got caught, and may suspect that you're now on tilt. (Reinforce this suspicion by making many tilt-like noises.) Even so, they won't expect you to drive-bluff again very soon because they know that *you* know you're likely to get called. When you bet, then, they ought to credit you with a real hand and fold. But they're damned if they'll let you resume your thieving ways so soon, and without a fight; using your own tilty behavior to justify their bad call, they'll go ahead and pay you off. Remember, these are ego-driven players, and their egos will take them places their wallets shouldn't go.

WHAT NEXT: Settle down. Circumstances have allowed you to steal some chips by masquerading as a maniac. You were lucky to have caught a real hand when you needed it, but don't push your luck too far. You *were* caught bluffing and you *will* get called for a while. Let the cards and the character of the table determine where your image pendulum swings next.

CAVEAT: Recognize the difference between fake tilt and real tilt. If you think you're *faking* tilt, but you really *are* on tilt, you'll try to push second-rate hands like first-rate hands and end up losing all your chips. In all instances, know your own mind, and don't let emotion rule—or ruin—your game.

These are only a smattering of available moves one can make in the BFM of a successful NLHE cash game session— what my malapropistically minded gym teacher used to call "the tip of the icebag." All good players have their own playbook, and draw upon it when the time is right. Can you think of (and list) some signature moves that you use?

>>

If you don't have a big enough brain to store these plays for easy retrieval (and who does, really, in these times of information overload?), it's a good idea to get in the habit of jotting them down when you discover them or discover yourself using them. You don't need fancy names. It could just be "the play that works against drunks" or "the way I slow down maniacs" or "how I remind myself to be aggressive." But the more such plays you have at your disposal, and the more you think in terms of having plays at your disposal, the better off you'll be.

It's also a good idea to go into each session with an eye toward implementing one or several of your set pieces. This will improve your game in several ways. For one thing, you'll be mixing up your play and increasing your unpredictability. Also, you can use this strategy to shore up weaknesses in your game. For myself, for example, I have trouble firing Doyle's famous second barrel. I just figure that if they called me on the flop, they're not likely to release on the turn. This can cause me to shut down on the turn and surrender to a bet on the river, a disastrous practice in the presence of attentive foes. Since I know I'm not always right about their having a hand when they call, I tell myself going in that *today I'm firing twice.* Not all the time, for sure; that would be reckless and stupid. But at least from time to time I'm going to charge ahead where I would otherwise cower out, just because I told myself in advance that I would. In this I'm giving myself a strategy and a plan for breaking a habit I know I need to break.

More to the point—most to the point—by planning and executing set pieces, you raise yourself above the herd mentality that most players bring into their NLHE games. You're thinking about the session as a whole and considering the long-term impact of all your moves. Your foes, meanwhile, are still just down there lurching from hand to hand. They become like infantry soldiers stuck in the mud while you bomb and strafe them from the safe confines of a stealth fighter.

And then when you're done, you take the money and run.

10

BREATHING OUT

♣ ♠ ♦ ♥

" 'There must be some way out of here,' said the joker to the thief," and while I doubt Bob Dylan was thinking about poker when he penned those words, the question does arise in winning and losing sessions NLHE alike: When is enough enough? I don't have to tell you about the allure of the next two cards, for OMHS, One More Hand Syndrome, is a documented phenomenon among realworld and internet poker players alike. In service of our overall successful cash game strategy, then, we have to give some thought not just to how we play the game well but how we stop playing the game as well.

Often this decision is made for us. Denizens of small clubs know that the one or two available games will break at or around a certain time, as players get tired or go broke, or the municipal code curfew kicks in. Even big poker rooms suffer attrition as the night wanes. At Bellagio or Foxwoods or Trump Taj, the wee small hours are a ghost world of cardroom diehards still posting blinds and placing bets while infomercials for the Ab Blaster play on the plasma screens, industrial strength vacuum cleaners prowl the aisles between silent slot machines, and footsore drink runners make their orbits with increasingly dispirited cries of, "Cocktails? House'll buy you a drink." I've been there; I know you've been there, too. It's part of every poker player's rite of passage at least once to lap the sun, and it just serves to illustrate the profound adhesive power of chair glue.

The problem is ridiculously compounded online, because there the game *never* breaks, and if you can't find action at pokerbeatsworking.com, the delights of pokersickforpoker.com are only a mouse click away. Recall the First Law of Chair Glue:

AN OBJECT IN A POKER GAME
TENDS TO STAY IN A POKER GAME
UNLESS ACTED UPON BY AN OUTSIDE FORCE.

We often apply this outside force going in. We tell ourselves that we'll stay in the game until traffic dies down or the dinner party starts or we have to go to work. Those who are ineffective at extricating themselves from cash play often stick to tournaments, especially online, because these come with clearly defined end points: You stay until your chips, or all your foes, are gone. Those who are fuzzy minded about all this stumble into cash games with no clear notion of how long they want to play or what they hope to achieve. They have some idea about playing for "a while" and winning (of course winning) "some amount." So the hours roll by and chair glue grabs hold and the outside force that drives them from the game is ultimately exhaustion or poverty or both.

Here's a thought: Before you sit down and play, know exactly when you'll stand up and go. This is a radical notion, I know, for it flies in the face of the received wisdom that tells us to "stay in the game as long as the game is good." But I have a feeling (and certainly know from my own experience) that the act of placing one's cash play in a fixed time frame is yet another way of applying the clear-eyed rigor and discipline that winning poker players have. Suddenly your poker play is not an indulgence or a recreation, but a planned assault on the stacks of your foes. You know when you're getting in, and you know when you're getting out. You have, in other words, an exit strategy, and even a cursory survey of military history tells us how useful those can be.

But you know this already. You know the dull ache of walking away from the table one lap too late, when weariness, sleep debt, lack of focus, ennui, or oxygen-debt stupidity have caused you to make costly blunders—blunders you *know* you wouldn't have made an hour earlier.

Fine. We've all stayed too long at the fair, ridden the roller coaster one too many times, and upchucked on our shoes. How long, then, is *not* too long? What's a reasonable duration for a sensible poker session? Having spent an hour breathing into the game, how long should you now devote to the payoff? Two hours . . . three? . . . ten? Unfortunately, that's not a question I can answer. Only you can answer it, in terms of how long you can maintain your focus, discipline, and, not insignificantly, good spirit. Externals factor in, of course: Is the game still good? Is the lineup still one you can beat? Has the table broken and everyone gone home? Be most interested, however, in your internal weather forecast. That needs to be sunny in order for you to stay.

But the weather can change in a hurry. I've seen—you've seen, everybody has seen—how one bad beat can put a player on tilt and send him down the road to ruin. When that bad beat happens to me, I often just leave. I'm just not confident that I can keep my spirit and focus high in the wake of it. Yes, I know I may be walking away from a game that is still profitable. Yes, I know I should be able to shrug off adverse outcomes, and mostly I can. But sometimes stronger measures are called for. The most directly effective exit strategy is: exit, quickly. Over time I've become quite adept at listening to the little voice inside my head that says, *Leave! Leave now before it's too late!* That voice is never wrong.

Do you have such a voice in your head? Can you heed it? Or do you ignore it? And if you do ignore it, why do you do so? I can think of a couple of reasons. One might be the spurious need to "get even." Another might be that the setback comes early in your session, when the poker itch has not yet been sufficiently scratched. Can you think of a time when you knew you should've gotten out, didn't, and came to regret it?

   >>

It was a $200 buy in NHLE game at the Bike. I picked up pocket aces on the first hand, got them cracked, lost my stack. Desperate to "get well quick," I overplayed the next bunch of hands and felted myself again within about ten minutes. That's when I should have left, but the prospect of aborting a short bad session seemed worse to me somehow than staying and losing. I suppose I thought I could "right the ship," but it was sinking beneath my feet, and in all honesty I knew that.

Mike Caro talks about passing the point of pain and entering a mental state where losing more money won't make you feel any worse than you already feel. My own experience of this is that while most big losses are gradual descents, it's also quite possible to blast past the point of pain in a heartbeat. Whether this happens after ten minutes or ten hours, it's a strong cue to get up and get out. Sadly, this cue is hard to see through the haze of pain, but that's why we grow our self-awareness: so that damage control becomes easier over time.

Annie Duke has an even more practical approach to this matter. Speaking of limit hold'em play, she recommends leaving any game in which you've lost more than 30 big bets. The estimable Ms. Duke reckons that 30 big bets is what a good player can hope to earn in a good session, and therefore can have the reasonable expectation of recouping her losses next time out. To go beyond that threshold is to dig a hole too deep, and not just in monetary terms. A big loss leaves ache in its wake, and the residue of that ache makes correct play more difficult during the next session.

Applying this paradigm to no limit, I would say that two full buy ins is a reasonable cutoff point. After all, on a good day of no limit play, you'll double your money, and on a great day you'll triple it or more. Having lost more than two buy ins yesterday, you might arrive for play today burdened by the need to have not just a good day but a great day. This need can make you press edges that aren't there and make plays that, well, just make matters worse.

It's quite possible that a temporary setback is just that, a temporary setback. If the game is still good, and your head's still on straight, then of course you're going to stay and play. It would make no sense to flee every time someone put a beat on you. But there's a deeper truth here: Sometimes you're playing like crap and you know it. At those times, your little voice of self-preservation shouts to be heard over a cacophony of rationalization. Listen to the little voice.

WHEN THE VOICE SAYS QUIT, QUIT.

If you're playing well, though, the question yet remains: "How long can I keep this up?" For myself, I figure I'm good for only three or four hours of topflight poker before my focus starts to fade. This may seem like a short span of time to you, and for you it may be, but I have a wandering mind. I can't do *anything* for too terribly long before I want to go do something else. This is just a fact of who I am. It's not a character flaw. Or rather, it's only a character flaw if I know about this limitation and refuse to acknowledge it, to the detriment of my performance and my profit. Professional athletes are known to say, "It's better to retire one season too early than one season too late." While I might think differently if I were drawing down their multimillion-dollar salaries, it's certainly true that in poker you want to get out before you go bad. To quote the sage,

THE TROUBLE WITH TOO FAR IS
YOU NEVER KNOW YOU'RE GOING
TILL YOU'VE GONE.

Remember, for recreational player and professional alike, part of poker's appeal is undeniably scratching that itch. Only you know how long it will take for the itch to be adequately scratched. For some players, two hours will do the trick; for others, two straight days isn't enough. So . . . know yourself. Your meticulously kept records will tell you how you fare in marathon sessions. Your gut will tell you when you've passed the point of diminishing returns—if you're open enough and honest enough to listen when you talk to you. In a cash game you always have the option to leave. Knowing when to exercise that option is one of a winning player's real strengths.

I'm not at all interested in "setting a profit floor" or "locking up a win," though I know many players who play that game. They get ahead, say, $300, and tell themselves that they'll leave if they drop back under $250. In some sense they imagine themselves to be playing with the house's money, but this (il)logic ignores the manifest underlying truth of poker that all of our play amounts to one long session. Individual outcomes don't matter, except in terms of how they affect us psychologically. And I suppose in that light you could make an argument for locking up profit: A win today, even a small one, may leave a given player better mentally equipped to play again tomorrow. Such a player, though, is treating the symptoms, not the disease. It's fundamentally misguided to be thinking about net plus and net minus. All that matters is performance. If performance is there, results will trend well. Trouble is, obsessive attention to outcome *kills* performance. The player who sets a profit floor, then goes through the floor and yet stays and plays is, of course, making a mistake; the player who sets a profit floor and leaves when he hits it, even though he's still playing well and feeling good, is making a mistake as well. This is why

I advocate letting the clock dictate the length of your session. If you're good for four hours, play for four hours. Then leave. You've done your work for the day.

However you go about setting a deadline, should you play differently as it approaches? In certain respects certainly not. You never want to throw away chips on reckless adventures just because you're down to your few last hands. Among other things, this may annoy you so much that you go on tilt and stay in the game—on tilt—even though you had planned to leave. More to the point, bad poker is bad poker no matter when you play it, and money lost is money lost whether on the first or last hand of the session. That said, there are a couple of parting shots you can fire off while you're breathing out.

FISHING WITH TRASH

If the game is sufficiently loose and passive, such that you can expect to see a lot of flops without taking a lot of heat, you can open up your endgame calling requirements to include a wide array of hands . . . stuff like 9-6 suited, T-J offsuit, tiny pairs, and bad aces, especially bad suited aces. These hands are playable now (and only now) because you're not worried about being tabbed as weak-loose. Yes, you are weak-loose, but you're weak-loose with a view toward flopping a monster and doubling through on your way out the door. This will be a strategic shift for you because as an appropriately aggressive player, you have probably inhabited the big fat middle by raising much more than calling preflop. You have been nurturing and projecting the image of someone who makes hands and also makes aggressive plays. Since you know you'll be leaving in a handful of hands, protecting that image now becomes unimportant. Were you to adopt this (flawed) strategy earlier in your session or throughout your session, you'd find yourself facing raises preflop and/or getting outplayed postflop by anyone at the table who recognized you as being too cally for your own good. As a late wrinkle in your play, though, you can make these highly speculative calls knowing that by the time your foes adjust, you'll be on down the road or, in the case of internet poker, logged off, shut down, and curled up in bed with a good book.

Let's draw a distinction, though, between speculative holdings and pure cheese. You can call with middle suited connectors or tiny pocket pairs because these hands have the potential (albeit slim) of getting hit hard by the flop and leaving you in command of the hand. And when they miss—and they'll mostly miss—they miss manifestly. It's no trick to get away from 8♣-9♣ when the flop comes A♥-K♥-Q♦. You still won't play death hands like 7-3, 6-2, or 8-4; what would be the point? Similarly, if you fish in with such up-down holdings as K-7, J-5, or Q-6, you're likely only to half hit, leaving you either with good pair, crap kicker or bad pair, okay kicker, neither of which is likely to delight you.

On the subject of up-downs, this would be a good time for a shout-out to my friend Russ Fox, who propounds the *Rule of 13*. I stand in awe of this rule because of its simple utility in helping me keep my head on straight, even when I'm frisking around at the end of a session.

> *The Rule of 13 says to add the blackjack value of your two cards (all ten-value cards are worth ten and aces are worth one). If they sum to 13, fold. The rule is a mnemonic designed to reinforce the idea that you should not play trash hands. If you fold your trash hands without thinking, you will be a step above many of your opponents.*[4]

When I'm breathing out, especially if I'm in late position and utterly unafraid of a raise, I might take a shot at 13s like 7-6

---

4. Russell Fox and Scott T. Harker, *Mastering No-Limit Hold'em* (Pittsburgh: ConJelCo, 2005), p. 56.

suited. In the main, though, I heartily endorse the Rule of 13; you'll never lose money following it, that's for sure.

When you're fishing with trash, your plan for the hand is simple: get in cheap; fit or fold; and play cards that can flop big, be clearly ahead postflop, and not vulnerable to redraws. That's a lot to ask for, I know, but what the hell? It's your going-away present, right?

Let's say you limp late with 9-7 suited. Someone raises out of the small blind. What do you do?

>>

Right, you fold. Okay, someone *doesn't* raise out of the small blind. Instead, four players take a flop, which comes down 9-8-6. It's checked to you. How will you proceed?

>>

This is a good flop for your hand, though not absolutely clearly the best hand. In a weak-loose milieu such as this, T-7 suited is possibly out against us, and J-T could be lurking, looking to hit the nut straight. Plus there is the usual assortment of potential set and two pair hits. So this flop is not *exactly* what we had in mind. Sitting in late position, then, you can either check, accepting the gift card, or make a utility underbet. The advantage of the latter course is that even a small bet might get the hand checked to you again on the turn. If the turn is a brick, you can take your free card then; if you hit, you'll bet for value. Your foes might credit you with A-9 suited here, and pay off your straight with two pair or a worse straight. That's what you're going for: a lightning strike with an unexpected holding.

But let's have no illusions about where we stand on this hand. We're out of line with a mediocre holding. Unless and until we hit again on the turn or river, we can't be sure we have the best hand, and should be leery of reraises. The point of this holding is to trap, not *get* trapped, and it would be a disaster to gut our stack on an unnecessary adventure. The thing is that our residual image (their picture of how we've *been* playing) no longer matches our approach. Our foes haven't seen us play junk holdings, and don't know that we've changed gears, so they may feel emboldened to bet both with hands worse than ours and on pure pot grabs. That's fine, we love that. But then again, they may have a set or top/top, in which case we're imperiled. If we're not driving the action, we must be certain that we're calling with the best of it before we get involved in a big stack confrontation here. The moral of the story, then, is

TREAD LIGHTLY WITH TRASH HANDS.

I'm not one of those players who restricts himself to the top of the deck. I've made too much money with surprise holdings—*because* they were surprise holdings—to ignore the value of playing trash from time to time. While I would encourage you to have the play of substandard hands as part of your repertoire, never forget that they *are* substandard hands. In such situations, you're dancing through a minefield. There's nothing wrong, really there isn't, with just giving the minefield a miss.

Another problem with trash hands is the toxic influence of wishful thinking. After all, you started with a plan for the hand: play crap and get lucky. Having gotten a flop that fit your plan, you bet along, anticipating a happy outcome on your nice little getaway play. But then some boho makes a monster raise and you're lost in the hand. You're lost because you can't be sure whether he's playing big cards or his flawed image of you. You're lost because you don't have the support of quality cards. You're lost because you're playing in a way that's unfamiliar and uncharacteristic. At this point, subjective reality sets in and you call because you've convinced yourself he's bluffing, or you raise because you've convinced yourself that you have to bet out of trouble. You don't have to call and you don't have to raise. You can *fold.* Cut your losses. With trash hands more than any other, you've got to be ready to bail.

BIG WIN FOR A LITTLE ACE

Here's why I hate little aces: because they're hard to bet unless you flop perfect, and you rarely flop perfect. In the normal course of a normal session, they score small wins when no one else has an ace—or large losses when they're dominated. If we're smart in the play of small aces, we don't get frisky when an ace hits the board, for fear of better aces. If we're smart in the play of small aces, we don't get frisky when *no* ace hits the board because then we basically have a solo overcard, and what's up with that? But I would ask this: If we're that smart in the play of small aces, why do we play them at all? The answer, I think, is that the sight of an ace—any ace—fogs the brain and trumps common sense. *That's an* ace! *That's the* best card! Hooray!

So bad aces are a known hole in most people's play. I hope they're no hole in yours. I try hard to make them no hole in mine, folding them both willy and nilly, unless the situation demands that I raise with them—in which instance the situation usually doesn't care what two cards I hold. But late in a session when, again, I'm not worried about protecting my image, I'll take a flier on a little ace, hoping to score a big win against someone holding a big ace. This requires an uncharacteristic flat call, out of position, against a kosher player who puts in a raise.

So right away you know it's a bad idea.

But when it works? Mmm . . . divine.

What we're looking for is to go up against a better ace and receive a gift. How unlikely is this gift? A♦-5♥ beats A♣-K♠ about 25 percent of the time and ties about 5 percent of the time. Seven times out of ten, then, we'll be on the losing end of this proposition. But wait, it's worse, because that 25 percent is a pure outcome based on seeing all five cards for the price of preflop action. That won't happen unless someone's all in or all parties are just rampant Timmies, content to check it down. The argument for getting involved with a bad ace when holding a short stack or going against a short stack is completely different; in that case you're betting that your hand is the best or has favorable pot odds. In the case we're discussing, we assume we have the worst hand going in, and know that if we don't flop perfect we're done with the hand.

With all that in mind, then, there's really no good reason to make this move.

Unless . . . you know . . . you want to.

If you do get involved, you need to weigh how much you stand to win if you hit your gift. The money has to be deep on both sides. Moreover, you need to be sure you're up against the right kind of foe, someone who will blithely bet her better ace, not credit you for two pair until it's too late—*and still pay you off.* Such foes are not that rare, for just as most players fall in love with bad aces, most players fall way too in love with good ones.

So let's lay out the gift scenario. It's a $5 and $10 blind game. You hold A-5, and your foe holds A-K. You're out of position, limp in, then call a raise to three times the size of the big blind. I truly don't know how you've gotten involved here. Maybe you've been possessed by aliens. Anyway, the flop comes A-5-3. There's $75 in the pot (your bets plus the blinds). You've got a grand, he's got a grand. How do you want to play it?

>>

What I like to do is check-call on the flop. I don't want to lead out, because I don't want to slow my foe down. Moreover, I have a plan for the turn that involves convincing him I'm either bluffing or betting with a worse ace. Remember, I need him to have a better ace here. So let's assume he does. I check. He bets $50. I call. There's $175 in the pot. The turn comes an 8. I love this card because it doesn't create any draws that might cause alarm, nor is it likely to hit a hand (A-8) that my known-kosher foe would raise with preflop. In short, he thinks it's not scary and I *know* it's not.

You could go for a check-raise now on the turn, but I think it's better to bet out. Remember that many out of position bluffs go check-call on the flop, then lead bet on the turn. If that's your betting sequence, you might convince him that that's exactly what you're up to, making a play for the pot. To check-raise, on the other hand, telegraphs real strength and may kill your action. As an alternative, you might check-call the turn and lead out on the river, but that's not the specific trap we're trying to spring here. What we really want is for our foe to put us on a worse ace, a middle pocket pair, or a pure bluff, and raise our lead bet on the turn. Many players holding A-K or A-Q will do this, since most of the time the hands they're facing are a worse ace, a middle pocket pair, or a pure bluff. This time, though . . .

You bet $150. He raises $300, figuring to drive you off your bluff or make you pay with your inferior cheese. You reraise—not all in, but enough to pot commit yourself. Sensing that it's you, not he, who has stumbled into a trap, he'll pounce on your "failure" to go all in by tapping you now. You, of course, happily call.

Most of the time we don't play bad aces this way. Most of the time we don't play bad aces at all. In unraised blinds or volume pots you might find yourself involved with a bad ace, especially a suited bad ace, looking for all sorts of possible outcomes, including good draws, flopped trips, and steal opportunities. Flopping two pair against a better ace is usually just one of many eventualities you're considering. In this case, it's the specific outcome you seek. If you get it, you're lucky. Very lucky. Yes, you put yourself in a position to get lucky, but it was a precarious position just the same. So *bonne chance* and *bon voyage*. Now go home.

OVERPAIR STACK ATTACK

It would be nice, would it not, to slowplay a big pocket pair and take someone off his whole stack as a little going-away present to yourself? The problem with slowplaying, though, is that it precludes protecting your hand and allows weaker holdings to catch up. A further problem is that it's basically passive activity, and does little to make you feared at the table. For this reason, the whole slowplay/trap scenario is not a habit you want to get into. But late in the day when, again, image is no issue, dialing back on a big pocket pair can put you in position to do serious stack damage if the flop comes right for your hand.

For this scenario, let's give ourselves J-J, that notorious hand of which it is said,

THERE ARE THREE WAYS TO
PLAY POCKET JACKS—
ALL WRONG.

Pocket jacks earn this reputation, of course, by being simultaneously not quite a big pair and not quite a small one. They're too strong to be played strictly for their set potential, and too weak to play ferociously as a monster. Raising with jacks is often wrong because it leaves you vulnerable to the kind of hands—A-K, A-Q, K-Q—that can call a raise and then easily hit the flop. Calling with jacks is often wrong because it lets inferior hands in for cheap. Folding with jacks is often wrong because, well, it's *jacks!* There's one thing pocket jacks do fairly well, though, and that's trap top pair/top kicker. That's what we'll be going for here.

By limping with jacks—or other pairs in the range from nines to kings—we encourage inferior hands, trappable hands, to join us in the fray. Let's say that in a $5 and $10 blind game we hold J-J and limp in from early position. Several callers later, there's $50 in the pot. As usual, if we don't get the flop we're looking for, we're gone, but this time the flop comes dreamy: T-6-3. In a sense, this flop is even better for us than J-6-3, for the hand we're trying to crush is top/top; and with only one other jack out there, it's much less likely that a jack on the flop will generate the action we want.

Now then, how shall we go forth?

>>

What we're hoping is that someone out there among the multitudes can be seduced into giving up his chips. We want this player to have a certain size stack: big enough to be worth winning, small enough for them to get careless with . . . let's say about $200 in this instance. Since we limped preflop to disguise our strength, there's no reason for a player holding top/top to believe that he doesn't have the best hand. To reinforce this misplaced sense of confidence, we'll check if it's checked to us, let top/top lead out behind us, then come over the top. If all goes according to plan, he'll have bet enough already—$50 or so—and be sufficiently optimistic to put us on a worse ten or a play at the pot, and call off the rest of his stack.

Many, many stacks are lost in this manner, for the seductive power of top pair/top kicker is great indeed. Players with that holding will often fail to give credence to the threat of an overpair, especially in the hands of a normally aggressive raiser who would be expected to have raised with such a powerful hand preflop. Naturally, this argues for mixing up your play, especially with hands like those problematic jacks. It also argues for caution when you're the one holding top/top. You don't want to give any foe the satisfaction, or the profit, of trapping you for your stack. Certainly you want to press top/top when you hold it, but not so brazenly that you can't get away from your hand in the face of major heat. This goes all the way back to knowing your foes. If you're on the receiving end of this particular check-raise, you need to know whether the person making the play is capable of doing so on a bluff. If not, figure you're beat and move on.

A move such as this, the overpair trap, need not be saved specifically for your endgame play. Any time you sense that your foes are insufficiently wary, you can dial back on your normally aggressive stance and look for a chance to hang them on their own optimism. What you're looking for, always, is a stack worth winning in the hands of someone careless in its defense. In other words, pounce on the unwary. Pouncing on the unwary is what NLHE is really all about.

I don't want to give you the impression that the last few hands of a session offer special license for negative expectation play—I'd certainly be leading you astray if I did. Negative expectation play has its place, mostly in the implied odds of taking large sums off bad players when your longshots come in. Against good players this won't work, for they'll be aggressive enough to punish you for your screwball holdings, and cagey enough not to pay you off when you hit. At that, it's never a good idea to get carried away with implied odds. Implied odds count a lot of chickens before they hatch. Nevertheless, at the end of a session, well, you can try a few moves.

What other ploys might you essay if you knew you weren't long for the game?

>>

Two final caveats for the breathing out stage of your game. First, if you're gonna go, *go*. The plays I've described will leave your image in tatters and leave you vulnerable to all sorts of strong moves. Don't stick around and be a victim. You planned to loosen up and then leave; make sure you do all of that, not just half. Second, manifestly, don't tip your intention to exit. If you're playing around to your blind, don't advertise the fact by packing up your iPod or racking up your chips in advance. Attentive players know that everyone gets looser when they're leaving. Most people loosen up becau0se they're looking for a last scratch of the itch before they split. You're loosening up for a different, strategic, reason, but you're loosening up just the same. Don't make yourself an easy target. Take them by surprise when you go.

PART III

TOURNAMENT
WONDERLAND

♣ ♠ ◇ ♡

11

THE TOURNAMENT MIND-SET

The only poker tournament I ever go to where people don't mind busting out is the one UltimateBet.com hosts annually in Aruba. There, the warm waters of the blue Caribbean and the mind-numbing powers of the blue agave quickly dull the ache of whatever savage beat or slow attrition sent you to the rail. When the rail is a beach, in other words, it's not so bad. Most of the time, of course, the rail is not a beach. It's the desert hotbox of Las Vegas, or the trackless wastes of Tunica, or the driver's seat of your own car where, rich in recrimination, you make your way back home. I'm not sure recrimination is called for, though. Sure, many tournament bustouts are our own damn fault: We overplay a hand, or let ourselves get trapped, or just get tired or careless or dumb. Often, however, busting out of a tournament has less to do with the quality of our play than with this simple fact of tournament Darwinism:

MOST OF THE TIME,
MOST PEOPLE LOSE.

It's true; it's the fundamental truth of tournament poker. From the smallest weekday nooner at your local card club to the biggest online poker mega event, the vast majority of people who enter any poker tournament anywhere come away empty-handed. In a ten person sitngo, 70 percent of the field gets *bupkis*. At the main event of the 2005 World Series of Poker, 5,069 out of 5,619 players received nothing more for their buy in than an interesting experience and maybe a bad beat story to tell. Even UltimateBet's Aruba tournament, with one of the deepest, flattest pay tables around, monies only about a fifth of the field. For everyone else it's, "Thanks for playing, don't forget your sunscreen." Despondence, then, is a completely inappropriate response to busting out of a poker tournament. Most of the time, you simply can't expect anything else.

Does this mean we shouldn't play tournaments? Of course not. For all sorts of good reasons, tournaments are good value. New players can see a lot of hands for not a lot of money, gaining crucial poker experience at a predetermined price. Even seasoned players appreciate the fixed downside risk of a tournament buy in. Better than average players who have a better than average chance of making the money in a tournament enjoy an overlay against the field. And for players at every level of expertise, tournament poker offers the lightning-in-a-bottle opportunity to turn a small investment into a large payday, possibly even a life-changing one. This potentially huge return on investment is simply not available in cash game play, and it's exactly the hope of the monster payday that brings so many people into, and back to, tournament poker, even though we know that most of the time most of us must lose.

What is it that brings you to tournaments? Are you there for fun? Money? TV glory? To jump-start your poker career? Whatever your motivation, you should be as clear and articulate about your tournament goals as you are about your cash game play, because it's never a good idea not to know *why* you're doing *what* you're doing.

>>

I play poker tournaments for the challenge. For the hours or days that they last, they test my intellect, stamina, fortitude, and skill. I like the definite sense of accomplishment that comes when I win. Cash game wins are nice, but they're indeterminate. When I defeat a large field to take down top prize in a tournament, I'm able to tell myself that, for this moment at least, I am the best. I like being the best.

These days, thanks largely to the explosive popularity of NLHE tournaments on television (and of course to the seductive popularity of the game itself), no limit hold'em has become practically synonymous with tournament poker. From endless website offerings to those weekday nooners at your local club to pro tour and circuit events, NLHE dominates all slates—so much so, in fact, that certain Grumpy Guses now complain that, for example, the World Series of Poker has become the World Series of No Limit Hold'em and has therefore somehow lost the purity of its roots. It's certainly true that NLHE has spread like kudzu, putting pressure on other, native, species of poker, but again, that's poker Darwinism, the people speaking with their buy ins, as it were. This is not a good thing or a bad thing, it's just a thing that is. Since I don't see a backlash to draw poker or a resurgence of razz happening anytime soon, I think it's fair to say that if you want to play tournament poker, you'd better know no limit.

No limit's no monolith, though. Within its realm there's a vast array of tournament structures and formats, including rebuy events and freeze outs; full table, short table, and heads-up matches; slow structures where the money starts out deep and the blinds rise gradually; fast structures where the opposite is true; team play; even turbo matches, where the blinds rise by the minute, and the event amounts to an adrenalating game of big stack truth or dare. Just as there's no one right strategy for all cash games, there's no one right approach to NLHE tournament play. But there are a few controlling ideas, and in this section I plan to touch on some.

I've already touched on one key idea: Most people lose. This doesn't mean that you should enter any tournament with the gloomy cloud of fatalism hanging over you. That's the worst sort of self-fulfilling (which is to say self-defeating) prophecy. But it does mean that you can exit any tournament you don't win—assuming you've played your best—with your head held high. If nothing else, you're in abundant company.

With that in mind, let's look at some productive ways to think about tournament poker; ways, if you will, to shift ourselves into the monied minority.

LOOK BEFORE YOU LEAK

True story. I go to my local cardroom to play in a NLHE tournament I've entered many times before: $100 buy in with one rebuy/add-on. I play my usual fearless-because-I-can-rebuy early round strategy and make it to the end of the rebuy period with roughly twice my starting stack. Before going off on a break, I plunk my add-on money down—only to be greeted by the dealer's vacant stare. "What?" I say. "I want my add-on."

"There's no add-on," she says.

"What are you talking about? There's always add-ons."

"Not anymore. The structure changed today. This tournament's a freeze out now."

Really? Goodness! I dodged a bullet I didn't even see.

The moral of the story is my favorite moral for stories like this: *Don't do stupid things.* More to the point, know what you're getting into. Apart from gross mistakes like thinking you're in a rebuy tournament when you're not, make sure you're equipped with basic information like how many chips you get to start, how quickly the blinds rise, and how long the tournament will last. This would seem self-evident, but it's not. For we who play many tournaments, the details do tend to blur. And even if they don't, they change. So hold your assumptions at bay. Take a moment to scan the structure sheet, if for no other reason than to assure yourself that you're getting into what you think you're getting into.

Apart from studying the structure, be mentally prepared to *accept* it as you find it. I've encountered, and I'm sure you have, too, whiners who complain that the starting chip count is too small or the rounds are too short or the blinds rise too fast to give their (alleged) skill edge a chance to manifest itself. While it's true that long rounds, deep starting stacks, and slowly rising blinds favor skilled players, these Gripey Gripersons miss the essential point, a point I made just now in the context of NLHE's tournament dominance: The structure as you find it is not inherently a good thing, and it's not a bad thing. It's just the thing that is. If you can't accept the structure and make appropriate strategic adjustments, then *just don't play.* Getting all glowery over the structure will just put you in a negative mind-set and degrade the quality of your play.

This talk of negative mind-set reminds me of another (sad but) true story.

It was a Sunday evening. I had had a full and satisfying day: brunch with friends, a nice hike; I even cleaned out the garage. Now, at seven p.m., I had settled in to play a tournament, one of a month-long series hosted by the local cardroom of my choice. While I fiddled with my chips and waited for the tournament to start, I eavesdropped on the conversation between two players next to me. They had both played in the prior night's event, made the final table around dawn, then gone home and slept all day. Now, refreshed and rested, they were back for more, back for another battle, which, if all went according to plan, would take them again through the night.

My heart sank. Here I was, arrogantly thinking I could play excellent poker all night after having done other stuff all day. (My muscles already ached from all the garage cleaning; my toe throbbed from where I'd dropped a box on it.) My competition, meanwhile, had prudently turned their days around so that this tournament was the first—only, really—thing on their agenda. Whose chances do you like in these circumstances? I didn't like mine, I'll tell you that. I was so dispirited, in fact, that I never really made any effort to play well at all. I won't say that I busted out on purpose, but the thought of dragging my weary ass through the midnight hours and into the wee smalls was more, somehow, than I could face.

You'd think I would have thought of that ahead of time. I hadn't.

I have since, though. These days I never enter any tournament that I can't enter with a clear head, full rest, and enough time and energy to play the thing right. Again, you'd think such thinking would be obvious, but it's not. People enter tournaments lightly. They do it all the time. They often do it in full knowledge that they won't have time to finish what they start, and rationalize this with the probability that they'll bust out long before crunch time anyhow. There's a technical name for people who think along these lines: *dead money.*

Let's not try to be thus dead, shall we? If you don't know how long the tournament will last, *find out.* If you won't have time to see it through to the finish, *don't start.* If you don't like the way it's structured or how long it runs or the color of the chips they use, *don't play.* Never enter another tournament again unless you're absolutely in it to win it. Such a commitment won't necessarily guarantee you success, but its absence will certainly bode failure.

12

EARLY DAYS—EARLY PLAYS

♣ ♠ ◇ ♡

EARLY ROUNDS, NO REBUYS

At the start of a freeze out tournament, the risk/reward ratio is all out of whack. In order to position ourselves well for the middle rounds, we know we need to accumulate some chips; however, the chips we can get our hands on now are not worth very much, and going after them could cost us our tournament life. This tough paradox typically evokes two classes of response. Some players, fearing early elimination, tighten up in the early rounds, restricting their involvement to big hands and (near) lock situations. These conservative competitors look to inaction to take them deep into the tournament, where, they hope, their early circumspection will be rewarded by later favorable looks. Other players, seeking to build a stack, push early and push hard, hoping that a combination of bully behavior and big cards will get them the chips they need. These green felt samurai would rather bust out early than make it to the middle rounds with a middling stack. Which path is correct? The answer lies in the tournament structure itself. In a nutshell:

THE FASTER THE TOURNAMENT PLAYS
THE FASTER YOU MUST PLAY, TOO.

Let's look at two different tournament structures and see why this is so.

A typical "slow" tournament may give you 10,000 in chips to start and rounds of 90 minutes or two hours in length. Figuring 20 to 30 hands per hour, you'll see somewhere between 60 and 120 hands during the first two (cheap) levels of play. Given that you'll pick up a hand containing an ace or a pair roughly one time in five, you can thus stay relatively patient, knowing that you'll get at least some good cards, and at least some chance to get involved with quality starts. Moreover, with a slow structure you have the real luxury of not getting involved at all: ample time to breathe in to the tournament, just as you would breathe in to a cash game. Within a few laps you'll have the other players dialed in, and know where real pockets of strength, ability, and creativity lie. You'll know whom to attack and whom to avoid. And just as in a cash game, the tightness of your early play will create a false image of your approach to the game, an image you can work against later when you open up your play. In tournaments with plenty of play, then, default to the viewpoint of Antonio "the Magician" Esfandiari:

PATIENCE IS PRECIOUS
WHEN CHIPS ARE CHEAP.

At the other end of the spectrum, a typically "fast" tournament will give you maybe 800 or 1,000 in chips to start—and while the blinds start smaller, they don't start *correspondingly* smaller. In a slow tournament, the first big blind may be one half of one percent of the starting stack. In a fast tournament, depending on the exact starting stacks and blinds, that ratio will be three to six times higher. The blinds rise faster as well, every 20 or even 15 minutes. So you have fewer relative chips to start and much less time to make your move. Waiting for premium cards? You might only get 30 or 40 hands before the blinds are high enough to imperil a starting stack that hasn't been able to grow.

Between these extreme examples are all sorts of tournament structures and all sorts of variable relationships among starting stacks, starting blinds, and level lengths. Before the start of every tournament, take a moment to calculate the cost of doing nothing. How long, in other words, can you afford to sit on your stack without getting involved? If you have long to wait, wait. If the pressure will be on you from, or nearly from, the outset, you'll need to open up your starting requirements and look to get involved. A good rule of thumb is the 20x big blind rule:

IF YOU HAVE AT LEAST
20 TIMES THE BIG BLIND,
YOU'RE NOT IMPERILED.

So if you start with 600 in chips, and the first blind levels are 5–10 and 10–20, you can make it through two levels without your original stack feeling real pressure. At the third level, though, when the blinds rise to 15–30, you hit that 20x threshold and must be prepared to make some moves.

There are two ways to start doing so. One is to become hyper-aggressive, looking to build pots and then take them away. This tack would have you raising in early position with middle pairs and in late position with hands like A-9 or K-Q, hoping to isolate against just one or two players, and then bet any flop you hit, or any flop everyone seems to have missed. The other approach, in broad strokes, is to look to turn the risk/reward ratio around by limping into pots with lots of players and getting excellent value for money. This will only happen at a certain sort of weak/loose table, where many players are paying the minimum to see the flop, and few players are raising. In such situations, you can call with speculative holdings like suited connectors, suited aces, and little pairs. If the cost of your call is low, relative to your stack size, implied odds can give you an adequate potential payoff.

Whether the tournament structure is fast or slow, remember to take your cue from your table, and to take whatever opportunities the other players offer. If they're generally too tight, you can play loose and play the bully. If they're generally too loose and aggressive, you can lay back and hope to trap. In all events, be sure you're seeing the players as they are, not as you wish them to be. Many players in fast tournaments, knowing that they have to build stacks in a hurry, will try to run over a table, only to discover that the other players simply will not cooperate by lying down. These fast players let their own need for speed put them in peril.

There's no need, really, to bash yourself against the unyielding shoals of uncooperative foes. Relax. Observe. The other players will always give you something to work with. They'll be too fast, too loose, too tight, too scared, too *something*. With this in mind, don't feel like you have to force the action. Rather, seize opportunities that present themselves. Be flexible, adaptable, responsive. In other words,

LET THE GAME COME TO YOU.

At this point I would ask you to think about your own approach to the early rounds of a tournament. Is there a method or strategy you favor, and how does this strategy take into account the relative speed of the tournament itself?

>>

You can see from this question, I imagine, that no one approach will work for all tournament structures. Nor do these plans necessarily apply when rebuys are involved. Let's look at those next.

EARLY ROUNDS WITH REBUYS

Consider a $20 tournament with 200 chips to start and initial blinds of 5 and 10. Since this structure puts every starting player at the perilous 20x-big-blind line, rebuys will naturally be immediate and plentiful. This is of course how such a tournament is marketed: with a cheap initial buy in but high hidden (to some) subsequent costs. Here's a snapshot of the tournament in question.

$20 buy in, $5 entry fee • 200 in tournament chips to start • 20 minute rounds • $10 rebuys = 500 in chips • single rebuy when at/below 700 in chips • double rebuy when below 200 in chips • single or double add on at first break: $10 for 500 in chips, $20 for 1,000

BLINDS	ANTES
5–10	
10–15	
15–25	
BREAK	
25–50	
50–100	
75–150	25
100–200	50
200–400	75
BREAK	
300–600	100
500–1,000	200
1,000–2,000	300
BREAK	
blinds/antes double every 20 minutes till tournament ends	

As noted, this structure virtually forces one to take at least a single rebuy of 500 chips right away—and since you can rebuy anytime you're at or below 700 in chips, many players take two rebuys to start, jumping their stack up to 1,200. Twenty minute rounds make this tournament play fast, and with rebuys priced at half the initial tournament buy in, all-in moves and big stack confrontations abound, and cries of "Rebuy! Rebuy! Rebuy!" echo out across the tournament floor. It's not uncommon for players to go six, seven, ten rebuys deep into the tournament in the first hour of play.

And then take all available rebuys and add ons before play resumes after the first break.

Naturally this sort of nose-is-open style of play requires some strategic adjustments on the part of sensible players like us. If, for example, you see people repeatedly overbetting inferior holdings like K-Q and A-6, you should definitely try to isolate and confront such foes. Isolating them may be a challenge, for the other sharks smell the same blood in the water as you do. Forcing a confrontation, however, will be a snap, for these players, protected as they are by the safety net of the rebuy, are just aching to go all in. Their bad aces will lose to your good aces and their low pocket pairs will lose to your high ones. It's as if, in a sense, they're buying your rebuys for you.

Likewise, the protection of the rebuy will cause loose players to play even looser, calling preflop raises with hands they should fold, hands like bad aces, suited kings, and unsuited middle connectors. Try to get involved in volume pots with good aces, bad suited aces, and pocket pairs. Look also to hit flops like two pair, and look to get paid off by top pair. This is another case of pouncing on the unwary. After the rebuy period is over, they'd never consider putting their tournament life on the line with top pair/bad kicker. They might even think twice about going to war with top pair/top kicker. But while the rebuy frenzy lasts, they allow themselves all sorts of promiscuous calls, knowing that they can always shout, "Rebuy!" and get back to gambling again.

Even while you're trying to exploit the mental weakness of others, you yourself should keep making good gambling decisions and not get torched by rebuy fever. When there's a bet, an all-in raise, and two calls in front of you, your A-2 is not the best hand and not getting proper odds to call, no matter how devalued the calling requirements of others. Per Rudyard Kipling, you want to "keep your head when all about you are losing theirs." Above all, you don't want to get so deep into rebuys that a $25 tournament ends up costing you $200 or more. At that point, you'll probably have to make it to the top five spots just to make your money back. This is called getting upside down in a rebuy tournament, and amounts to giving an overlay to the rest of the field, letting others profit at your expense.

So how much should you budget for this rebuy tournament? Figure about $65, thus: Even the most aggressive (and lucky) player will rarely build a stack bigger than 2,000 or 3,000 in chips during the first hour of play in this tournament. While this will place him among the chip leaders after three rounds, it's not *that* dominant a position—not when everyone can reload through rebuys and add ons. Suppose someone didn't even show up at the table until near the end of the third level of play. Her starting stack of 200 might have been blinded in half or so, but at that point she just takes two rebuys and the available double add on. Having spent $65, she resumes action after the break with more than 2,000 in chips. The player who built his stack up to 2,000 or 3,000 before the break can only take the add on, not the rebuys, and so can only improve to 3,000 or 4,000 in chips. With blinds at 25 and 50 after the break, both a 2,000 chip stack and a 4,000 chip stack have sufficient room to move, so the big stack is in a leading, but, again, not all that dominant, chip position.

All the wild play during the rebuy period, then, is often

mere recreation (called by some the *fuckaroundarama*). You can't really go to school on your foes' play, because everyone plays differently—significantly tighter—after the rebuy period ends anyhow. Nor can you convey meaningful early (mis)information about your own image. For this reason, many sensible players don't bother showing up till near the end of the rebuy period. They figure that their chip position will be good whether they play or not, and they don't risk getting upside down in the event. While I validate this strategy, for myself I prefer to show up on time and treat the first hour of play as warm-up: an opportunity to dial in my own mind-set and get my game head on straight.

In almost all cases it makes sense to buy as many chips at the break as you can. This has to do both with maintaining your stack size relative to other players and also with the size of the blinds when play resumes. While 1,500 in chips might be adequate when blinds are 15 and 25, as soon as they rise to 25 and 50, and then 50 and 100, that size stack will simply not do the job. Twenty-five hundred chips will stand you in better stead, buying you the time you need to withstand a run of cold cards or hot opponents until you find profitable places to get involved. Not to take the add ons here would be a case of false economy: Yes, your investment in the tournament would be lower, but your chances of building a significant stack would be lower—perilously lower—as well. So while it's not a good idea to get upside down in a rebuy tournament, it is a good idea to include rebuys and add ons in your tournament budget. Don't be misled by the low initial buy in, for it doesn't reflect the real tournament cost. To play a rebuy tournament correctly, you must plan on strategically accepting the additional ammunition on offer. If you find that the accumulated price of reloading is more than you want to pay or can afford, simply give the tournament a miss. Rare is the rebuy tournament winner who gets there on the cheap.

One time to consider not taking the maximum available reload is when doing so will not increase your stack by more than 20 percent. If you get to the first break with the (admittedly rare) monster stack of 5,000 in chips, say, adding another 1,000 will only grow your stack to 6,000—and not significantly improve your chip position vis à vis either the other players or the blinds.

At the other end of the spectrum, if you've already put in lots of rebuys—if you're upside down in the tournament or risk being so—and still find yourself at or near the felt when the first break arrives, you may also decide to take a pass on the reload option. While I'm no fan of fatalism, I think it's worth admitting that some days you just don't have it. For whatever reason—lousy mood, poor focus, indiscipline—there are times when it's better to cut your losses, rather than throwing good money after bad (performance).

In the main, though, if you're in a rebuy tournament, consider the cost of rebuys and add ons to be not optional but necessary to correct tournament play.

13

THE MIDDLE KINGDOM

The middle rounds of a tournament are when the class of the field starts to emerge. Anyone can make it to the middle rounds of most tournaments—mostly by doing nothing at all—but prospering in the so-called Middle Kingdom and emerging into the late stages with a chance to win the thing, this is the stuff of real ability. For one thing, the dead money is gone. Those players who are unable or unwilling to protect their chips have had them swept away and forfeited to stronger, abler players, from whose hands it becomes relatively more difficult to pry them loose. For another thing, unlike in cash games, where straightforward play can take its time to grind out a profit, the cost of inactivity becomes sufficiently high in the middle rounds of a tournament that mere selective/aggressive play alone cannot protect most stacks from the scourge of rising blinds. At this point, one needs to be imaginative, intuitive, and bold.

For a remarkably concise précis of the skills required for tournament success, we turn to an unlikely source: former Los Angeles Dodgers pitching great Orel Hershiser. He and I were sharing a poker table once at Bellagio in Las Vegas, when the subject turned to what it takes to be a pitcher at the major league level. "With one pitch, like a great fastball," said Orel, "you can compete. Add a second pitch, like a curveball or slider, and you can win. It takes three working pitches, though, to dominate." I instantly saw that what he said applied to poker tournaments, too.

What's the first pitch? What's the first important cornerstone of poker wisdom that every tournament player requires, and initially acquires? Answer: *hand selection*. Master just this one aspect of the game and you can compete. Once you learn, for example, not to get carried away with A-Q or K-J, you can play appropriately tight and extend effortlessly into the middle rounds. You won't necessarily win, but you won't shoot yourself in the foot.

The goal, of course, is not just to compete but to win, so here comes the second pitch that a tournament poker player can hurl: *aggressiveness*. The hallmark of winning tournament players is their ability to fearlessly bet it up, extracting maximum value from good cards, putting pressure on their foes, and stealing more than their share of pots. Wed hand selection to aggressiveness, and you have a pretty dandy poker package. With these two "pitches" it's possible to navigate the Middle Kingdom and position yourself for a tournament win, at least from time to time.

If winning's not enough for you, if you want to dominate and crush your foes, the third pitch you'll need is *reads*. When you have the ability to put excellent reads on your opponents, then your hand selection and your aggressiveness cease being blunt instruments and become tools of finesse. With excellent reads, you can choose your starting hands more effectively, and choose from a wider array of them, for you'll know more precisely where you stand against your foes. With excellent reads, you can direct your aggressiveness at the right targets, regardless of the cards you hold. With excellent reads, you can get away from hands, make tough laydowns, and wriggle out of traps that would leave other players broke and staggering to the rail.

So there you have it: the wisdom of Orel Hersheiser, interpolated into tournament poker. Anyone with a modicum of card sense can more-or-less correctly choose which hands to play and, thanks to that, penetrate deep into the tournament field. To win requires aggressiveness, bully behavior. To dominate—and you see this all the time in the players who routinely win big tournaments—requires a perfected sense of what your opponents are up to.

HAND SELECTION
AGGRESSIVENESS
READS

Looking inward for a moment, ask yourself where your strength lies in terms of these three skills, and where you could stand to improve.

>>

Reads, of course, are more than just a matter of looking for tells or detecting patterns of play. Since the middle stage of a NLHE tournament is fraught with underlying psychology—it's the time where players start to *hope* to win and *fear* to bust out—the key to great reads really lies in deducing from available information *how your opponents feel right now.*

They could be feeling all sorts of things. They might be appropriately relaxed and carefree, determined to play their best poker, no matter whether they crash out on the next hand or make it all the way to the final table. Alternatively, they might be overinvested in a money finish, and will tighten up incorrectly for fear of busting out short of their cash goal. They may be intimidated to find themselves so deep in the tournament, especially if they're newbies in marquee events. They could be fatigued, and fatigue may leave them inattentive and open to attack. Perhaps they've become frustrated with a run of bad cards and are now starting to panic in the face of rising blinds. If they're short stacked, they may have lost hope and are now prepared to felt themselves on any old prayer.

What other states of mind have you noticed, or might you expect to find, during the middle stages of a NLHE tournament? What states of mind have you felt?

>>

Penetrating your foes' state of mind should not be hard. You will have been playing with these same players for quite some time, and they will have revealed much about their level of tranquility, depth of knowledge, starting requirements, relative discipline, and more. In fact, the only way you could *not* have excellent reads on your opponents is if A) they're very adept at concealing their true nature, B) your perception is clouded by your own negativity or fatigue, or C) you're just not paying attention.

The controlling idea for most players in the middle rounds of most tournaments is *fear of failure*. Having come so far, and invested so much time and money, they now sight the goal: a money finish. This awareness of (and urgent need for) a potential payday grows more and more acute as the money bubble nears. And where is your head at now in this respect? Just as other tournament players will start to think in terms of protecting their investment, might you also be falling into the trap of mere survival? If you are, you won't be able to use your reads effectively, for your own inhibitions about putting your tournament life on the line will block you from correct play. Remember,

ONCE YOUR TOURNAMENT FEE IS PAID, *IT'S GONE!*

It won't cost you any more money to bust out on the next hand than it would've cost you to bust out on the previous hand, and it won't cost you any more to bust out on the bubble than to have been the first one gone. While those around you are clinging to the desire to make the money, it's an excellent time to start letting go of yours. If it helps you, bear in mind that, over the long haul, the largest collection of low money finishes won't make you a profitable tournament player. Since most players (including you) don't make the money most of the time, the only way to overcome the sad math of tournament poker is to collect your share of top payouts. The infrequent first, second, or third place finish pays, as it were, for the many, many, many failures and false starts (and low money finishes) of tournament poker.

So mark your mind-set in the Middle Kingdom. Even if you have Orel Hershiser's famed three pitches, you're going to need one other element as well, and that's the will to win. Paradoxically, having the will to win means not fearing to lose. Further to the paradox, if you've made it to, and through, the middle rounds of the tournament, you've been at this task for many hours, or possibly days. Your focus may be frayed, so keep taking your internal weather forecast. If you feel yourself getting slack or lax, get away from the table and slap yourself in the face a few times. Orel Hershiser knew how to close out a game—that's why they called him Bulldog. You'll need that same mental toughness to finish as strong as you start.

14

WINNING THE DARN THING

As a no limit hold'em tournament progresses, it takes less and less of a hand—but more and more sense of where you're at—to take down the pot.

Early in the tournament, you generally need to show a real hand to win, for the field is large, loose money is yet present, and players are willing to gamble for the sake of building big stacks. To prosper here, you want to make sets or better, in order to take down the multi-way pots common in a tournament's early phase. Also, without being paranoid, you want to be wary of your foes' trapping tendencies, for big hand traps are common in volume pots.

During the middle rounds, as tournament tightness and survival strategies kick in, fewer players compete for each pot, and so hand values correspondingly drop. At this point, pairing the board is usually sufficient if you're willing to bet any piece of the flop, and so win pots from your (few) foes who swing at the flop and miss. The big danger here is the imaginative player who can reraise your steal attempt with nothing, but if you have your foes pegged as straightforward, you can probably lay claim to any pot you see fit to bet at.

In a tournament's terminal stage, the blinds and antes rise so high that heads-up, all-in confrontations become the norm.

At this point you often don't need to improve on your initial holding, as the best ace or the lone pocket pair is enough to claim the pot. Stack size is key, for players' calling requirements fall in inverse proportion to their sense of desperation. A bet or a call from a large stack is much more significant than similar action from a small stack: not just because a deep stacked player can break you, but also because a deep stacked player can afford to be patient, and so you must ask yourself why she's choosing to get involved just now.

This idea of sinking hand values should guide your actions as the money bubble approaches and passes, and the final table arrives. Here are a few other strategic notions to keep in mind during your transition from merely participating in the tournament to actually winning the darn thing.

ZIG WHEN THEY ZAG

As the bubble looms, most players naturally tighten up. For reasons previously described, they're yielding to the natural tendency to want to see *some* return on their investment of money, time, skull sweat, and luck. If you're in it to win it, and unafraid to swing your stack even at the risk of busting out, you can profitably swim against this tide by opening up your playing requirements while everyone else is shutting down theirs. To help you with this just remember that a low money finish is usually not much better than breaking even, and if all you had wanted to do was break even, you could have stayed home.

OPEN MORE POTS

Because players are now reluctant to mix it up with less than premium hands—and because premium hands are relatively scarce—you should look to open more pots for a raise when it's folded around to you preflop. Obviously you'd like to be able to do this in late position, but often someone else will seize that initiative before you have a chance. For this reason, look to make steal raises from earlier positions. This may actually increase the likelihood of success for your steal, since others will credit your under the gun raise with being much stronger than a button raise would be. Yes, they'll play back at you from time to time, but the combined high blinds and antes make this move profitable, especially considering the image equity your apparent fearlessness earns.

Say you raise to three times the size of the big blind on three straight hands. The first two hands you win without a fight. The third hand, someone comes over the top and you have to fold. Your net profit for the three hands is zero—but your image "earn" is significant. You have established yourself as a relentless, aggressive player, which might earn a free pass in your blinds, plus plenty more steal opportunities.

BET MORE THAN CALL

Fold equity is huge during tournament crunch time, and you simply can't earn any of that by calling along. Whenever possible, be the first one in the pot, and be in with a raise. Even if your bet doesn't win you the pot right there, leading the action often lends credibility to your hand (whether your hand deserves it or not) and gives you "the right of first bluff." Your foes are wary right now—too wary, probably—and any flop that comes the least bit scary will seem to them to have hit your hand when you hit the pot again. If they all fold you don't have to get lucky—and that's what fold equity is all about.

AVOID CALLY CONFRONTATIONS

By the same token, even if you think your foes are big lying liars, it's often a good idea to surrender the pot to them, especially when you're not imperiled and can easily afford to do so. There are so many endgame opportunities to win without the best hand—with the pure willingness to bet alone—that any calls you make that aren't pure traps should be regarded, and therefore eschewed, as reckless adventures.

FIND THE SWEET SPOT

When I detect strong pre-bubble reticence on the part of others, I start to look at any unopened pot as an invitation to get involved (and a license to steal). While their tightness will often yield me the results I want, I'm also mindful that promiscuous raising is a pretty clear signal of my strategy. If I raise too often, other players will quickly figure out that I don't have to have a hand, and start coming after me. So I look for the "sweet spot," a raising frequency that's plausibly reflective of a run of good cards, and yet not so relentless as to telegraph my thieving ways. In such circumstances I'm more attuned to the question of whether the *time,* rather than the *hand,* is right for a raise. Finding the sweet spot, then, is a matter of tuning your raising frequency so that your foes can reasonably conclude that you're raising with a real (or anyway realish) hand, and prudently get out of your way.

AVOID BIG STACK BATTLES

When you have a big stack late in the action, be very reluctant to mix it up with other big stacks. You can easily see why: When big stacks tangle, they risk running into catastrophe and running themselves out of contention. Nor are such confrontations necessary. With just two or three dominating stacks at a table (with, say, two or three tables left in play), each big stack has plenty of lesser stacks to attack without ever going head-to-head against the players who could potentially break them.

BE CIRCUMSPECT WITH SMALL STACKS

If big stack clashes are déclassé, then small stacks are the logical target, right? Not necessarily. Per Bob Dylan, when they've got nothing, they've got nothing to lose, and so will be willing to call you with A-2, K-J, or any pocket pair. Yes, attack small stacks, but not wantonly. Try to get in there with good aces or middle pocket pairs, hands that will prove no worse than a coin flip—and possibly a big favorite—against most hands that short stacks will call with. It's true that there's some value in busting small stacks, and therefore moving up in the pay table, but there are a lot of other players out there who can help you do the job. You don't have to do it all by yourself, and you certainly don't want to let a small stack get well at your expense.

PRESSURE MEDIUM STACKS

Consider the plight of players holding middling stacks of about 15 big blinds. They're not so short as to be desperate and reckless, but yet not so deep that they can afford to wait too long. They're in a pickle of a sort, and you want to make their bad situation worse by putting them to hard choices. Torment them with your raises, for it's their natural tendency to be optimistic about unseen cards; they hope that a judicious fold here will be rewarded with monster cards on the next hand. Therefore, attack stacks that are worth defending because, paradoxically, these are the ones that most players feel like defending the least.

TUNE YOUR RAISES

Late in the tournament, you need to adjust the size of your preflop raises to account for the presence of antes, and also for the number of people at the table, a number that will fluctuate as players bust out and others are shifted in. With this in mind, take a moment before every hand to *count the pot*. Know exactly how much is going in before the cards are dealt. Then, if you're coming in for a raise (and it's unlikely that you'll be doing much limping at this point), plan on opening the pot for the sum of the antes and blinds. This will ensure that the blinds aren't getting the right price to call, and yet won't leave you overinvested if someone plays back at you and you have to release your hand. That said . . .

LOOK AHEAD

Generally speaking, any time you have at least 20 big blinds, you're in reasonably good shape, and need not feel immediate peril. But what are 20 big blinds now will be just ten big blinds at the next level of play, possibly just a few minutes away. So always look ahead and always be aware of how long you can afford to be inactive. You don't want to let yourself get blinded down to a small stack, ever, but neither do you want to emasculate your stack through abortive adventures. It's a delicate dance, I know. You can't afford to be inactive, but you can't afford to be active ineffectively.

Try this: Whenever you contemplate getting involved in a hand, ask yourself what will happen if you have to break off your drive. If the consequence of bailing out will drop you below ten big blinds, therefore putting you into push-and-pray territory, don't get involved in the first place. If you do get involved, you must be confident that they'll fold, or else be willing to go to the felt with the cards you currently hold.

THINK LONG AND HARD

Whether you're playing in a realworld tournament or online, it's axiomatic that the tournament endgame is a time of fatigue. You've been concentrating hard for anywhere from several hours to several days, and if you think you're not tired, well, that's probably just the tired talking. Decisions that are automatic when your brain is fresh become problematic as weariness sets in. The only solution is to slow down your decision making and take the time to think things through. You don't want hours or days of perfect play to go to waste because of one careless snap decision or momentary lapse of reason.

GO BIG OR GO HOME

Two things get you to the final table: skill and no small amount of luck. Finishing first in the tournament likewise takes skill plus luck. How could it be otherwise? Skill may have carried you far, but you always have to make or call at least one all-in bet in the end to win. With that in mind, now is not the time for cold feet. Final table appearances are rare. Leverage your good fortune and good performance by going strong through the final table. Recognize that at least some of your foes will be content to coast upward through the pay places. Their timidity will give you another opportunity to zig while they zag. Seize that opportunity. The worst that can happen is you bust out. The best that can happen is Dame Fortune smiles on you and rewards you with a tournament win.

DO A DEAL (OR DON'T)

At the final table of an NLHE tournament, the offer to make a deal will almost inevitably arise. Because the money is bunched at the top (two-thirds to three-quarters in first and second place alone) and because players have worked so hard and gotten so lucky, many don't want to let the chance of a significant payday slip through their fingers. With blinds and antes climbing so high, sensible players would sensibly rather not risk their tournament equity on a coin flip, so they seek to flatten out their variance through dealmaking. Other players, equally sensible, want nothing to do with deals. Maybe they cherish the pure triumph of beating the whole field fair and square. Maybe there's a trophy or an all-around points prize at stake. Maybe they're just cussed-minded. That's fine. There's no law that says anyone has to strike a deal. Nor would I necessarily argue in favor of it. Certainly to an outsider's perspective, dealmaking can look like collusion and seem to taint the outcome, especially in this day and age when the game we love is under such pop culture scrutiny. Just imagine the foursome atop a PGA leaderboard getting together and agreeing to carve up the prize pool before the start of Sunday's play. It would be absurd on the face of it. Yet poker tournament players make deals every day.

It's because of the luck, of course. If you've reached the point in a tournament where pretty much everyone is going all in on every hand, the tournament's "winner" will be the player who gets the right cards at the right time, regardless of skill. When first place can pay ten or 20 times as much as tenth place, the argument for dealmaking starts to take on a logic of its own.

If you desire to deal, you naturally don't want to get taken advantage of, so you'll want to know what a fair and equitable deal would be. Fortunately, though dealmaking can seem to be quite arcane, we can actually boil it down to a simple three-step formula.

First, earmark for everyone the next place money (e.g., the payout for tenth place if there are ten players left; for third place if there are three left; etc.) and subtract that sum from the remaining prize pool. Second, calculate each player's percentage of the total chips in play. Third, dole out the remaining prize pool according to those percentages.

For example, let's say we have four players left at the World Series of My Basement Poker Classic. There's $500 left in the prize pool and one million total chips in play.

Fourth place pays $40
Third place pays $75
Second place pays $130
First place pays $255

Here's the current chip distribution:

SMOKER has 400K, or *40 percent* of the chips in play
MIRPLO has 50K in chips, or *5 percent*
CHINPEPE has 250K in chips, or *25 percent*
SUZZY has 300K in chips, or *30 percent*

We start by carving out fourth place money for everyone: $40 each, for a total of $160. That leaves $340 still to be divided and added to their $40.

SMOKER gets 40 percent of $340, or $136, for a total of $176
MIRPLO gets 5 percent of $340, or $17, for a total of $57
CHINPEPE gets 25 percent of $340, or $85, for a total of $125
SUZZY gets 30 percent of $340, or $102, for a total of $142

This method will determine a fair distribution of chips except in cases where the chip leader has so many chips that her equity is higher than first place money. At that point it would make no sense for her to deal, though it would certainly make sense for the others to try to bring her on board.

Which brings us to this: While there is such a thing as a fair deal, you don't necessarily have to settle for one that's merely fair. Many people who make it to the final table of a poker tournament are there for the first time; they may have no idea what a fair deal is. Others are so bent on locking up a decent win that they'll willingly take the worst of it. Some are just tired and they have had enough. Others fear they're outclassed by the remaining field and look to save both money and face. For these and many other reasons, a shrewd negotiator can tilt the final tally far in his or her favor.

Is it cricket to take advantage thus of the willing and the weak? Why not? Outthinking your opponents in dealmaking is just like outthinking them with bets and raises; it's all part of poker. You might, for example, propose an equal split even though your chip position is inferior. It never hurts to ask. Who knows? They might agree. Also, if you're of a mind to propose a deal, especially when the blinds are prohibitive, do so just before your big blind, when your stack, and therefore your negotiating leverage, is at its peak. Some of your foes may see through this ploy—but not all of them. Again, it never hurts to ask.

As in any negotiation, the willingness to walk away from the deal is your ultimate leverage. If you're up against someone who fears to be outplayed or outlucked in the tournament's final hands, your (temporary) refusal to deal could earn you a nice overlay. If worse comes to worst, you can always play the tournament out—and win the darn thing outright.

TAKE THE WIN

I have this thing I call my whole-life résumé. Where a job résumé lists employment history, my whole-life résumé lists all the things I've done that have made my life rise. It includes such items as writing books, marrying the woman I love, traveling to faraway lands . . . and winning poker tournaments. This is what attracts me to tournaments, really. Cash game wins are great, but they don't look nearly so good on the whole-life résumé.

For every tournament I've won, I've been aware that luck had a lot to do with it. With this in mind, I'm always both proud and humble with my tournament wins: proud to have triumphed, yet humble in the knowledge that it wasn't all my doing. When you're fortunate enough to win a tournament, be sure to savor your triumph. Don't be so focused on gearing up for the next tournament, or tipping the floorman, or fighting off the railbirds that you forget to *take the win*; that is, relish the moment you find yourself in. The money's great, it really is. But it's the thrill of victory—and the line item in your whole-life résumé—that really makes the trip worthwhile.

PART IV

♣ ♠ ♦ ♥

SCRAPMETAL AND DOUGHNUTS

15

NOTEBOOK

It's something I preach: Keep a notebook, keep a notebook, keep a notebook. It's a notion I flog until the dead horse is beaten, resurrected, and put back down again. I'm just such a believer in the utility of making your own discoveries in poker, and in a rare case of practicing what I preach (unlike, say, having starting requirements or not bluffing into large fields), I actually keep one, too. When I'm writing a book like this, my notebook becomes a repository for observations I make at the table, or topics I want to cover, or just the flotsam and jetsam of my idle mind. I'd like to share some of that detritus with you now, along with appropriate amplification, but before I do, let me remind you just once more: *Keep a notebook!* It'll focus your thinking and make all of your poker play more insightful, productive, and yes, profitable, too.

CARD HYGIENE

I'm sitting in the seven seat, out on the starboard wing. From where I sit, I have a clear look at seat one—who has one of the most self-destructive habits I've ever seen at a hold'em table. He's shuffling his hole cards . . . tilting them . . . and exposing them to this whole end of the table. As you can imagine, this makes him pretty easy to beat. While I wouldn't go out of my way to peek at another player's cards, I wouldn't go out of my way to avoid it. Poker is a game of information. When someone flashes his cards, he's giving away information for free, and for this he has no one to blame but himself.

Always practice good card hygiene. Cup your hole cards in your hands, glance at them quickly—*memorize them*—then lay them down, cap them with a chip or a card protector, and never look at them again. This may seem self-evident, but especially for players making the transition from online to realworld play, it's an issue of no small importance.

Realize also that looking at your cards can give away information even if you don't flash them. If the board comes heart-heart-heart, say, and someone checks their cards again, it takes no genius to put them on one or no hearts. If they had two they'd know it—people remember when their cards are suited. Probably they have one big card, the suit of which they didn't pay much attention to before the flop because they didn't think suitedness would be a factor. Now that you know your foe has one or zero hearts, you can go ahead and pressure him, for you can be certain he doesn't have a made hand yet.

Can you think of other instances where the way someone handles his cards could clue you in to his holding?

>>

* * *

THINGS I'LL DO

Much as I try to play my game with rigor, I often find myself doing things at the table that astonish me. I note these

TIDs (things I'll do) just to know what I'm capable of. While it's possible to assign a value judgment to these things (smart, stupid, brave, cowardly, psychotic), I'm much more interested in noting the thing than in judging it. In my experience, knowing that a thing is flat-out stupid won't necessarily keep me from doing it. But knowing that I'm capable of doing something will at least keep me from taking myself by surprise. As it's my goal to play poker all the time with conscious control, I need to know, and note, where control breaks down.

Here's a thing I'll do: Limp late with A-9 offsuit, which I don't think is all that smart, for in the cash games I play in, people limp with better aces all the time. I'm really hoping to flop two pair, and that's a longshot, no? Now here comes the flop of A-7-2, and the big blind comes out firing. With four players to act behind her, I can't put her on a bluff. Can't put her on a draw, 'cause there ain't none. I have to put her on a better ace, a set, or two pair, so I fold. So that's two things I'll do: play bad aces; and get away from them. I don't consider it correct to limp with that A-9 (can't curb all my atavistic urges) but if I do find myself involved, I'm not likely to get too enthusiastic about flopping an ace. In all events, I'd rather fold early and be wrong for a small sum than be wrong late at catastrophic cost.

What are things you'll do?

>>

* * *

FOLDING IS A STRENGTH OF MY GAME

I feel I'm pretty adept at getting away from a hand. I don't chase when the odds don't warrant, and I don't squander a lot of cash or tournament chips on loose calls when I know I'm beaten. If it sounds like I'm bleating my own horn, I'm not . . . exactly. I'm just acknowledging, for the sake of reinforcing, something I know I do well. (There's plenty of stuff I know I don't do well. Essaying huge bluffs for large sums, for example, is definitely *not* a strength of my game. And I acknowledge that, too.)

If folding is a strength of my game it's because I'm honest and frank about the situations I find myself in. I don't let regret or desire color my thinking. I don't cling to a hand solely in hopes that the other guy is bluffing. Occasionally he is, of course, but if I put someone on a draw and the draw gets there, I won't then turn around and put him on a bluff just to keep from having to surrender my investment in the hand. When I'm beat, I'm beat. I fold and move on. It's a strength of my game (though sometimes I have to remind myself it is). What's a strength of yours?

>>

* * *

FURTHER TO FOLDING

In most games, against most players, the correct preflop action is *fold*. Arrogance occasionally makes me think otherwise, because sometimes I feel like I can outplay anyone. But in most games, against most players, cards are more important than the spurious ability to "outplay anyone." Or let's put it another way: If you're in a game you can't beat by straightforward selective-aggressive play, JV, you're probably in the wrong game.

In most games, against most players, the next most correct action is *raise*. It's the aggressive part of selective-aggressive. If I find myself flat calling a lot, that's a clue to me that I'm off my game. It means I'm too weak to play strongly, but too loose to fold correctly. I'm playing hit-to-win poker, and I *hate* that. A sharp spike in my calling frequency is a reliable indicator that tiredness or tilt has arrived.

* * *

THE TAUTOLOGICAL TRUTH

Postmodern no limit hold'em theory makes arguments for playing across the whole deck, and not limiting one's involvement to top cards only. The rationale goes like this: If you're never in there with surprising (i.e., junk) holdings, how can you ever trap the unsuspecting and take them off their stacks? While this argument holds some water, it ignores the simple math of the matter: High cards win more than low cards do. Moreover, if you're in there with T-6 in hopes of flopping two pair and snapping off a stack, where will you be when the flop comes A-T-6—and the other guy has A-T? At some point we must return to tautological basics:

GOOD CARDS GOOD.
BAD CARDS BAD.

This is especially useful if you're new to no limit or (as often happens) you've lost faith in your game. When all else fails, snug up your starting requirements, even at the risk of playing too tight or too predictably. You'll stay out of trouble that way, and build up your experience and your confidence, from which healthy platform you can later make those junk hand forays that lend nuance to your play and, in all fairness, take it to a higher level. But like the saying goes, you have to learn how to walk before you can pitch forward on your face.

*   *   *

LET THE GAME COME TO YOU

I get into trouble when, through impatience, tilt, or the afore-mentioned arrogance, I try to force things. I need the patience of an alligator. I need to sit and sit and sit and sit . . . then *strike!* I'm more likely to have this patience if I've allocated sufficient time to play the session correctly. I'm also more likely to have this patience if I'm ahead in the game, or at least not behind. I know that individual outcomes don't mat-ter, but I need constant reminding. For me, for anyone, it's easy to feel the need to get well, get even. I think that the ability to absorb a loss is the strength of strong players' games. I'm just not sure it's a strength of mine.

*   *   *

THE RELATIVE NATURE OF TIME

Blinds fly when you're having fun.

*   *   *

MY STYLE DEFINED

Someone asked me to describe my style of play, and in my whimsy I came up with "swoop and pummel." This phrase was the motto of the Santa Barbara Condors ultimate frisbee team, and I've always admired the confidence of it. What does it mean to swoop and pummel? I guess it's another way of saying pounce on the unwary. In this imperfect world of ours, especially in the brave new world of no limit hold'em, flaws abound in our foes. If we take time to identify those flaws, we can give ourselves ample opportunity to swoop and pummel. This is about picking off top/top with overpairs. This is about getting loose and cally players stuck on their draws. This is about laying rope-a-dope on inveterate bluffers. This is about taking what the game gives you. The game gives you plenty if A) you don't try to take what isn't there and B) you're bold enough to strike when opportunity knocks.

How would you define your style? In your whimsy, put it into words.

>>

*   *   *

PLAY THE GAME YOU'RE IN

Not the one you wish you were in. Tonight I faced a lineup that wouldn't let me establish my game. Every time I raised, I got reraised. Every time I tried to bluff, I got called. Somewhere along the line I realized that there was a disconnect between the foes I faced and the ones I wanted to face. I wanted a table I could dominate, but that wasn't the table I was at. So I dialed back my aggressiveness, screwed down my starting requirements . . . and, most crucially, hunted for another game.

To find a game I could beat, I had to drop down from the $300–$500 buy in table to the $100 buy in table. Such is often the case. I do much better in a smaller game I can

dominate than a larger game where I can't get a bet in edgewise. Friskiness is a strength of my game. I like to see a lot
of flops and make a lot of moves. This strategy, which com-
plements my style and proclivity, works well in small games,
but not so much in bigger ones, where bigger egos and bolder
souls than mine have already claimed the friskiness high
ground.

In the main, I have no trouble playing small. I play poker for
recreation, and with recreational sums. I take my pleasure out
of playing the game correctly, and take great pleasure out of
outwitting my opponents. I would much rather play well against
bad players than play poorly, and feel frustration, against good
ones. At this moment I'm reminded of a key poker teaching:

DON'T CHALLENGE STRONG PLAYERS, CHALLENGE WEAK ONES— THAT'S WHAT THEY'RE THERE FOR.

The fact is, it's hard to play well against good players.
That's what makes them good.

* * *

MISTAKE HUNTER

When boredom becomes a problem for me, and I feel myself
turning too loose because of it, I turn to a little game I call
mistake hunter. After I've folded my cards I watch everyone
else to see if I can pick off any mistakes. These might be
tells, or transparent bluffs, or calling without proper odds,
or checking the nuts, or just the garden variety bonehead
poker I see every day in the places I play. I keep a running

tally, and while there are no prizes for high score, I do keep trying to top my personal best. This is just one of the myriad strategies I use to curb the urge to play too many hands.

Poker players think that the only interesting thing to do at a poker table is play hands. Over time I have found that there are many other interesting things to do. I have names for these games within games. *Mistake hunter* is one. I also play *ghost*, where I try to guess what cards someone holds. Then there's *tell popping*, where I try to correlate tells to actions. Needless to say, all of these games have the benefit of increasing my awareness of my foes, but I really only do it because I'm so easily bored. What do you do when you're bored?

>>

*   *   *

PRETEND YOU'RE ON TV

I've played a little on TV, and it scares the crap out of me. The thought of the whole world out there second-guessing my decisions really takes me off my game. I know this is a mistake, and I know that more TV time would probably make my jitters go away. For now, though, I have to be on guard, and not come off my game on camera.

Being a TV poker commentator, I've had plenty of opportunity to view things from the other side of the lens. I've found that most players do what I do: tighten up. The pros don't. They've been there before and are not nonplussed ("plussed," would one say?). But for the rest of us, well, it's easy for our fifteen minutes of fame to skew our composure.

But you can turn it around, you know. Even if you're not on

TV, there's some value in pretending you are. Especially on-line, where our anonymity protects us from the humiliation of getting caught being stupid, it's easy to fall into bad, careless habits. To solve this problem, just ask yourself, "Would I play that hand that way if the whole world were watching?"

The dividend is discipline.

*   *   *

A POEM

. . . Titled *That's the Last Mistake I'll Ever Make.*

Ha.
As if.

*   *   *

FLAWLESS AND FLAWEDFUL

Here's the thing about tournaments: You can play 300 hands flawlessly and then one hand flawedfully, and be bounced right out on your ass. So when you get deep into a tournament, go ahead and take pride in your good play and good fortune, but don't get carried away. In improv comedy there's such a thing as "shining," where you become more interested in being impressive than in being part of something successful. The same thing can happen in tournaments, and the better we play 'em, the more at risk we are for catastrophic meltdown.

It's not enough to say, "Stay focused." Anyone can say, "Stay focused," and anyone can think they're focused when really their thinking has gone all fuzzy. This is beyond focus:

Wed yourself to the tournament mind-set where nothing matters—nothing!—except playing these two cards correctly. Go to school on your Phil Iveys and your Chris Fergusons. They never lose their equipoise. They're always stable as a table from the first hand to the last hand—which explains why they're there for so many last hands after all.

It's no tragedy to bust out of a tournament. Happens all the time. The tragedy is to squander an opportunity with loose thinking or carelessness. Being in it to win it isn't just about capturing the top spot. It's also about being worthy.

* * *

THE MANIAC'S MANTRA

Life's too short to wait for the big blind.

* * *

CALLING ALONG

There's something to be said for calling a raise in position. Many players will raise preflop and then bet out on the flop. Far fewer will bet again on the turn if they get called on the flop. If you're up against someone who follows this pattern, go ahead and call along behind them, almost regardless of what you have. If the flop comes unfavorable to a raising hand and they bet, go ahead and call again. When they check the turn, they're indicating that they've shut it down and they're just begging to have the pot taken away. Generally I'm no advocate of just calling, but in position behind a predictable player is one time you can profitably do so.

* * *

BE NOT AFRAID TO LOSE

Note to self: Be not afraid to make big bets in big situations. If I'm afraid to lose, I'll make the wrong decision. I'll check when I should bet, fold when I should call. Why? Because the prospect of *losing*, and especially *losing big*, is more than I can bear. So be not afraid to lose, JV. Be not a cowering coward.

Easier said than done, right? To inspire myself to correct play, I use the Fortune Cookie of Fearlessness:

IN THE PRESENCE OF FEAR, NOTHING IS POSSIBLE. IN THE ABSENCE OF FEAR, ANYTHING IS POSSIBLE.

This doesn't necessarily cure me of the dreadful cowers, but it reminds me that there is an alternative to playing nimrod poker. At minimum, if I'm not afraid to lose I set myself apart from, and above, those around me—and they abound around me—who are.

* * *

PLAY EVERY HAND KNOWLEDGEABLY

If you can't do that, don't play. This is yet another argument for breathing in to a poker game. How can you possibly expect to play every hand knowledgeably when you don't know your foes?

* * *

EVERY PLAYER IS A PUZZLE TO SOLVE

Don't assume they're more complex than they are. Especially don't assume they're trickier than they are. A bet is usually an indication of strength. Treat it as such until you have evidence to the contrary.

* * *

MOOD MANAGEMENT

You have to be in a good mood all the time at the poker table— even if you're not. Apart from the fact of mood management (you play better when you're happy), there's the appearance factor. If you seem to be all glowery, the other players will be inspired by your gloom, attack you for it, and make it that much harder for you to achieve your goals in the game.

So, to borrow a mantra of recovery (and are we not here talking about recovery of equilibrium?): "Fake it till you make it." Or maybe we should turn to our friend the Buddha, who endowed us with true poker wisdom some 2,500 years ago when he taught "right action, right mind." According to this concept of inner mental trickery, if you can't be happy, you can still be sham-happy. And even if they don't buy what you're selling—even if you don't buy what you're selling— eventually your thoughts will catch up to your deeds, and you *will* play happy again.

It also helps to have plenty of tiltproofing rituals on hand, things that you know will help lift you out of your grim mind-set and back up to Happy Camper Land. Some of these strategies are well known, such as taking a break or taking a walk or knocking off for the day. One thing I do to get happy again is remind myself that bad times at the poker table are just a luxury crisis; that only the privilege of income, leisure, and circumstance allows me to be in the game in the first place. "The worst day of poker . . ." right?

Also, when I'm feeling like my game is sick and will never get well, I find that I can "borrow confidence" from some other part of my life where things *are* going well, and apply it back to my poker. This is more than just thinking happy thoughts. It's reminding myself of what it feels like to feel good. Even the act of writing something down can restore my mood, as I tell myself, "Well, you may have been so stupid as to call a big reraise with a bad ace, but at least you're smart enough to know it and note it and own it." That's the start of the road back to balance.

Can you think of any tiltproofing rituals that you use or might use to salvage the wreckage of your drowned mood?
   >>

*   *   *

PREMEDICATED MURDER

A poker move planned under the influence of drugs.

*   *   *

CB OR NOT CB, THAT IS THE QUESTION

Sometimes I can win a pot by *not* making a continuation bet. Here's how that works. I raise in late position with anything at all and get one caller. The flop comes T-9-3. My foe checks to me. Should I bet? Let's assume that she knows me (or thinks she knows me) well enough to figure me for overcards. In other words, the flop missed me, and she knows it. If I CB, she'll put me on a pure steal. Plus, if she's on a draw, she might stick around, raising the possibility that I'll be bluffing into a made hand on the turn. So what I do (when I don't think the CB will work) is check behind her and take a free card. Specifically, I'm looking for phantom overcard outs: any ace, king, queen, or jack. Since I could easily have raised preflop with A-J or K-Q, any overcard can look like it hit a hand I'd raise with preflop but not feel comfortable about continuation betting on the flop. If my foe checks, I'll bet, and figure to win the pot right there.

Of course, I'm alert to the possibility of being trapped or resteal-bluffed. (Though by this point in the session I should know whether my foe is capable of these things, should I not?) And if the turn comes low I will refrain from betting, by the same logic as not making a CB on the flop. Nor will I be afraid to check this hand down if the situation warrants. I don't worry about showing CB reticence. I love them to know that I'm capable of raising with nothing and then not following through with postflop bets, since this is not the norm of my style and will muddy the waters of my real intentions and approach.

An added benefit of running this program is that it controls the pot size against draws. Many players will chase draws on the flop (even though they shouldn't) when they still have two cards to come. By waiting to bet the turn, I deny draws both the right price to call and the optimism of that second card. Now they're down to just one shot at their draw and the pot is yet small enough to surrender.

By not making the expected continuation bet, then, I put

myself in a favorable position to win the pot on the turn in situations where I might not be able to win it at all on the flop.

* * *

SOMETIMES IT FEELS LIKE THIS

I have no fear. Unfortunately, I also have no clue.

* * *

LIGHTNING RODS

Some players have a disproportionate impact on the play at their tables. We might call these players LRs, lightning rods, for the way they attract action. An example of this would be a player during the rebuy phase of a tournament who goes all in at every opportunity. While such promiscuous raisers frequently get upside down in the tournament by making too many rebuys, they can also infect others by causing them to loosen up their starting requirements and all in requirements as well.

Say you're up against one of these LRs who has shown a willingness to call all in (during the rebuy period) with something like A-6 or K-J. You can certainly gather some chips by pushing all in with your good aces and medium-to-large pairs. In the nature of NLHE, though, sometimes you're going to end up on the losing side of your favorable proposition, and will find yourself rebuying perhaps more than you intended. So beware the seductive quality of LRs. They can be profitable, but also dangerous. In fact, any time you're responding too much to the actions or antics of another player, it's wise to pause and contemplate his impact on you. Is he presenting you with a real, exploitable profit opportunity, or just distracting you and taking you off your game?

* * *

TABLES WHERE YOU CAN'T MAKE MOVES

We pride ourselves on our trickiness, and we count on our repertoire of moves to provide us with profit. There are times, though, when the table is immune to our moves, and we have to default to straightforward kosher poker, or else find another game. Tables like this are ones where the players are either too strong or too weak. When the players are strong—which is to say incisive and bold—they'll see through our moves and play back at us. When the players are weak—which is to say clueless and ill-informed—they won't read our moves as moves, and therefore won't do what we want them to do. Recall Mike Caro's warning against Fancy Play Syndrome and remember that strong play is wasted on the weak.

* * *

A CLUE TO REAL ABILITY

With so many NLHE players learning so much about the game and its basic selective-aggressive strategy, it's no trick to find players strong enough and well informed enough, say, to make a button raise for the sake of picking off the blinds.

That's garden variety no limit skill among today's well schooled players. But when you see someone making a limp-reraise from early position, you know you're in the presence of higher caliber play, for the limp-reraise takes not just education but also thoughtfulness, imagination, and guts. Further, since the limp-reraiser will be out of position throughout, it requires a bold and considered plan for the hand ahead. A player who's capable of this move, then, is one worthy of respect . . . and caution.

Are you capable of this move? Do you ever limp-reraise with a big hand? Have you ever limp-reraised on a naked bluff? Try it next time you play. Sure, it might cost you some chips, but you'll gain some image equity, and some inner image equity as well. You'll see yourself as a player who has thoughtfulness, imagination, and guts.

Plus, of course, you might win the hand.

* * *

TRAIN YOUR FOES TO GIVE YOU FREE CARDS

Try to make a noisy check-raise at some point, or try to be especially noisy about your check-raises, in order to communicate to your foes that it's not necessarily safe to bet behind you when you check. This is another example of stealing position. If you demonstrate a little recklessness up front, you may have your pick of free cards later.

* * *

AN ALMOST CORRECT IDEA

Many tournament players root for chips to accumulate early in the hands of weak players, the logic being that it'll be easier for us good players to pry them loose later. While this is a realistic attitude, it's not sufficiently confident for my taste. Here's the notion I would promote instead:

THEY'RE ALL WEAK
HANDS BUT YOURS!

If that sounds dangerously arrogant, let me temper it thusly: Against every player, no matter how strong, there is an effective winning strategy. Your job is to learn and adapt (with confidence and without arrogance) so that no matter where the chips accumulate, you can figure out a way to pry them loose.

Let's say the player to your left is weak and has chips. You can grab some of them by flat calling in the small blind and outplaying him after the flop. Since he's weak, he won't bet hands he doesn't have, and will therefore surrender more often than not. On the other hand, if the player to your left is strong and has chips, you can raise from the small blind, knowing that this player is strong enough to respect your raise and get away from his big blind. This strategy becomes very important when blinds are high and the tournament is reaching the tipping point where the gain or loss of just one blind can make the difference between winning and losing the thing.

To reiterate a familiar idea, *take what they give you.* They're always giving you something.

* * *

DUMB MONEY

A lot of times, in both cash games and tournaments, the presence of dumb money can make you feel rather smart and cocky and confident. Win a few pots from bad players and you start to think you've got the game figured out. However, in tournaments, and to a lesser extent cash games, the dumb money can disappear rather quickly. Remember always to update your take on the players around you. Among dumb money, it's possible to play recklessly successfully. Against smart players, that's a recipe for disaster. Shifting gears, then, is not just a matter of adjusting according to your own plan, but according to the changing lineup, too.

*   *   *

BAD (TABLE) BREAKS

One of the worst things that can happen in a tournament is to have a table completely under your spell . . . only to have it break. Suddenly, the players you were dominating and crushing have been scattered to the winds, and you yourself are plopped down at a table full of strangers—strangers who have already figured each other out, but who are all unknown quantities to you.

At this point, a certain seductive logic can creep in. Since they don't know you, you reason, you're free to run any kind of moves you like at them. They don't know you, so they must fear you, right? Not necessarily. While you may be carrying with you to the new table a very strong internal image (your sense of how you're playing), you carry no *external image* at all. Plus, you may find yourself up against players with very strong internal images of their own. Against these players, your new-kid-in-town bully moves will be met with fierce, possibly catastrophic, resistance.

Recognize, then, that your first few minutes at a new table are hazardous ones, and take your time breathing in to the table as you would at any other. Of course you may not have the huge luxury of time, since your chip situation might be putting pressure on you. But even a quiet hand or two spent studying where the table strength lies will help you make a successful transition to the new table.

* * *

THE BANE OF BAD ACES

You can't push with them, for fear of betting into better aces, but you *can be pushed off* them, for fear of calling better aces. Easier to avoid the whole big mess and just not get involved in the first place. This is a luxury you can *always* afford in cash games, though not necessarily in tournaments, especially late.

But even late in tournaments, bad aces are bad news, particularly when you're going all in. Whether you're betting all in or calling all in, the hands you're most likely to face are good aces, unpaired paint, and middle to big pocket pairs. And bad aces perform poorly to terribly against these hands. They have a small edge over unpaired paint—but unpaired paint is the *least* likely holding you'll face. Against dominating aces or tweener pairs, bad aces will falter, crash, and burn.

* * *

WHEN THE MONEY GOES IN THE MIDDLE

In cash games when someone goes all in, top/top should not be good enough to win. If it is, it's because someone did something wrong. After all, what hands *do* top/top beat? Top pair/worse kicker; middle pair; busted draw; naked bluff.

If top pair/worse kicker calls an all in bet, it's because he didn't fear a better kicker.

If middle pair calls, it's because he didn't fear the bigger pair.

If busted draws call, they're just being silly.

Naked bluffs never can call—that's not a bluff.

Before you shove all your chips in the middle, ask yourself if your foe is flawed enough to make the big mistake of calling you when calling you would be a big mistake. If not, don't bet, for you'll only get called if your top/top's no good.

*   *   *

THE DANGER OF BOTTOM TWO PAIRS

You're in the big blind and you get a free ride with 6-2 offsuit. The flop comes 8-6-2 and you're feeling like, *merry Christmas!* You check-call to disguise your strength and a king comes on the turn. Now you blithely bet out, only to be raised all in. How do you like your chances? In the best of circumstances, you're up against someone who thinks her K-J or K-T is good. In the worst case, you're up against K-6 and drawing dead to a deuce.

I'm not saying you should play scared with bottom two pair, but do recognize what a fragile holding it is. Especially if you get involved in an unraised pot from the big blind (and how in heck *else* would you get involved with 6-2 off?), be aware that there are likely to be other garbage holdings besides yours in play. A lot of players love to limp with half-hands like K-8 or J-T, just for the sake of snapping off the unwary. *Be* wary. Don't let your excitement about, like, *merry Christmas!* keep you from seeing things as they are.

Can you think of a time when you got felted with bottom two pair? Was there any way you could have avoided that trap?

>>

* * *

TWO THOUGHTS ABOUT CHANGING TABLES

A) If you've got a bad feeling about a table, there's usually a reason why—and even if there's *no* reason why, the bad feeling should be enough to make you change, for how will you play well at a table you have such a bad feeling about? B) If you're in the right game, there's no need for tricky moves, and if you're not in the right game, *why are you still there?*

I recognize that changing games is not always an option in the realworld, but it's *always* an option online, and if I spend a single moment in a game that's too fast, too big, or too rough for me, I have no one to blame but myself.

* * *

A NOTE ON BREATHING IN

Never be frustrated by your self-imposed patience, and never consider it a punishment not to play hands. There's so much to look at and so much to study. But here's the thing: You shouldn't be concentrating *hard*, you should be concentrating *easy*, taking everything in with a lightness of spirit that says, "Now I'm learning, soon I'll be winning, and that's as it should be." With so tranquil a mental stance you will be virtually unassailable.

* * *

HOMEWORK

It's useful to go into every session with a homework assignment in mind, such as running a scare card bluff or raising your own big blind with trash or anything that takes you out of your comfort zone. Why? Because it takes your foes out of theirs as well. If you play things safe, you make things safe for others. Get feisty!

Can you think of some homework to assign yourself today? >>

* * *

DON'T BE A FUNDRAISER

Some players have the flaw of raising preflop with a wide variety of hands, but then shutting down if they miss. While promiscuous continuation bets have their threats, if you routinely fail to deliver postflop pressure, you become just a fundraiser—someone who builds pots for others to win.

* * *

THE CONFIDENCE CONUNDRUM

If overconfidence is a problem and underconfidence is a problem, how do you find the sweet spot of just exactly balanced confidence? By stepping outside the confidence equation altogether. Confidence is not the controlling idea; dispassion is. It's okay to note where you are on the confidence scale (from terribly Timmy to absolutely arrogant) but that's not the root of your actions. Act because it's correct to do so, not because you feel strong enough to do so.

* * *

LOSING FOCUS

Losing focus is losing everything: discipline, perspective, caution, dispassion, and the ability to look within and without. What else do you lose when you lose focus?

>>

Sadly, this can happen worst in the best games. When the players around you are such Mirplos that you can't wait to take their money away, impatience sweeps over you, focus evaporates, and you become a Mirplo, too. Sometimes "not playing down to their level" is simply a matter of not being greedy. Relax. Let the game come to you. If they're truly bad players, they'll surrender the cheese—so long as you don't surrender your focus first.

* * *

DECEPTION AND DELUSION

"Deception," as we know, "is what you do to others. Delusion is what you do to yourself." It's delusion, not deception, then, to dignify a trash hand by calling it a "variation raise." There's nothing wrong with variation raises, and even nothing wrong with playing the occasional trash hand—so long as you're doing these things honestly. Always examine your motives. Are you making a move because the move needs making or just because you need action? Always note the difference, in other words, between strategy and self-indulgence.

*   *   *

IT'S NOT ABOUT THIS HAND, BUT YET IT IS

It's never about this hand. It's only about long-term expectation, not specific outcome. However, it *is* about this hand and it's *always* about this hand, in that you have to play this hand correctly in order to achieve positive expectation.

The long run is now.

It always is now.

*   *   *

THE TRAIN WRECK

When I'm playing badly and know it, it's like I'm watching a train wreck unfold in slow motion. I see it happen—am fascinated by it—but seem powerless to stop it. I see myself just looking for a chance to get involved with something like A-J, make a complete hash of the hand, and lose all my chips. Then it happens and, well, I couldn't say I'm surprised.

The only antidotes to the train wreck are screw-tight play and lower levels. Oh, and not playing at all. That'd probably work, too.

* * *

BAD CARDS ARE ONLY PART OF THE PROBLEM

Games where you're not involved in a lot of hands are probably not profitable games. Why are you not involved? Bad cards are part of the problem, but it's more likely that you're just being dominated by someone, or several other someones, at the table. We all want to play tight. It's great to play tight. But how can you make money just sitting on the sideline? If you can't ever get a bet in edgewise, where are your offensive weapons? In sum, if the real or perceived strength of your foes is taking you off the strength of your game, it's time to look for that ol' table change again.

* * *

HOW ARE YOU RUNNING?

"How we're running" is a function both of the cards we're getting and the way we're playing, and we can represent it graphically thus:

GOOD CARDS PLAYED WELL	GOOD CARDS PLAYED BADLY
BAD CARDS PLAYED WELL	BAD CARDS PLAYED BADLY

Profit is likely when you're playing good cards well. Profit is still possible when you're playing bad cards well or good cards badly. But watch out for the moronic convergence of bad cards and bad play. That's not a hole you're digging; it's a grave.

* * *

OF CHOPPED BLINDS

You know you're in an action game when the question "Do you chop?" is entirely rhetorical.

* * *

BLACK EMOTION

A stray thought can cause bad decisions. I was thinking about a mistake I had made away from the table—in a whole other realm of my life—and almost made a ridiculous call with 9-2. Fortunately, or through practice, I had enough self-awareness to detect the underlying *black emotion* motivating my call: Something inside me was hurting, and something told me that playing a hand of poker would somehow ease the pain. This is a familiar root cause of tilt, and the fact of it is no surprise to anyone with even modest poker experience.

Nor must black emotion necessarily come from other realms. Bad beats, bad luck, and bad play can all bring it on. Recognizing the onset of black emotion—nipping tilt in the bud—is a skill worth cultivating. You can resolve to be as dispassionate as hell, and try to hold yourself in place with all the rigors of your discipline, but averting tilt is not about discipline, it's about awareness, plain and simple.

Know yourself.

See yourself.

Accept yourself.

Everything else flows from that.

* * *

A RECIPE

For mediocre results, play mediocre cards.

* * *

IN THE CARD DESERT

Sometimes you go so card dead that you feel like you're wandering in a card desert. Beware of mirages here. Look at enough 7-2 offsuits, and that Q-6 suited will start to look like pocket aces. If you find yourself making "oasis raises," it's probably time for a break.

* * *

ON FRISKY PLAYERS

I'm not sure there's much edge in trying to put frisky players in their place. You can trap 'em, sure, but driving them off their steals . . . why bother? The fewer small pots you contest, especially when someone else is driving and even when you think they have crap, the better off you are.

Further to this, in fixed buy in NLHE games, where the name of the game is building a big stack and then using it to capture other big stacks through traps, there's really no reason not to let the bullies bully away. Participating with them in marginal situations for small pots is simply irrelevant to your goal for the game.

* * *

THE TOURNAMENT BUZZ

Of course you're amped when you sit down to play a tournament. Your body knows it. You may be shaking or sweating or, like me, really chilly. This will pass, of course, once the tournament gets well under way. Until that happens, recognize that you're under the influence of the buzz, in this case the hope of a big tournament win. You're treasure hunting, really, and treasure hunters do get amped. So breathe in to the situation. Let your body do its thing.

And if you're like me, always bring a jacket along.

* * *

A PROBLEM FOR THE RISK AVERSE

Let's say you've got top/top on the river. There was a possible flush on the turn, but the river bricked out. Now a loose, frisky player checks in front of you. Should you bet for value here, hoping that she'll pay you off with a worse hand? Or should you check, figuring that she won't call if she was on a draw? The problem with value betting into a frisky player is the real risk (for the risk averse) that by opening the betting you'll invite a monster reraise that puts you to a hard choice. Generally, then, if you know that your foe is capable of big bluffs, deny her the opportunity, even at the cost of a little extra value.

* * *

ANOTHER REASON TO BREATHE IN

When you join a new NLHE game, you don't know what's the going rate for raises. Will a min raise fold the field? Will over-betting the pot just trigger a call fest? How big must your own raises be in order to accomplish your goals? These are things you can't know at first, and must learn through observation. Since information is power, wait till you're fully empowered before you fully engage.

* * *

THE SADDEST THING IN NO LIMIT

Counting down your stack to ship it when you lose.

* * *

WHAT IT AIN'T ABOUT

It ain't about pride. It's about profit. It ain't about dignity. It's about dollars. It ain't about the buzz. It's about the bottom line. If a smaller game offers a larger edge, *play there.*

* * *

VERBAL SPIN

Sometimes you like to put a little English on your bets, some verbal spin designed to get the outcome you're after. Occasionally this will work. If you know enough about your foes to manipulate them, you can talk or taunt them into calling or folding to your big bets. But predictable players will play predictably—and, again, game selection should routinely put you up against such foes. They either have a hand or they don't, and will either call or fold accordingly.

Still, it doesn't hurt to try. As Caro points out, if you want a call and it looks like they're going to fold, do something, *anything*, to try and change their minds. You have nothing to lose, and potential profit to gain.

* * *

HOW BIG IS ONE PAIR?

Against one foe, it's huge. If you flop a pair and the flop has no aces or kings, and not more than one queen, jack, or ten, you're probably in great shape. Go ahead and hit this flop with a bet. Obviously, if you encounter resistance you should slow down, but a gratifyingly large percentage of the time, you'll win the pot right there. Recognize this also as a bluffing opportunity. A flop like Q-3-2 is very hard for someone without a queen to get excited about—and most of the time your single foe will not have a queen.

Even a flop like K-J-6 can work in your favor against a certain form of foe. Let's say he has a jack, but you come out betting. Look how easy it is for him to put you on a king and make the proverbial "good laydown." If aggressiveness is rewarded in hold'em generally, it's profoundly rewarded one-on-one.

* * *

A HERETICAL THOUGHT

There's really no such thing as a tight NLHE game—at least not for long. The minute the game goes snug, someone will see fit to exploit and attack its tightness. Such attacks will not go unnoticed, of course, nor undefended for long. Soon everyone is engaged, and the game has loosened right up. Consider, then, that the game you're in is always somewhere on a constantly swinging pendulum from tight to loose to tight to loose. Where is it now, and where is it heading? You can deal yourself some profitable opportunities just by getting out ahead of the curve. For example, start out stealing when others are tight, and then tighten up—and trap— just before the others go loose.

* * *

UNDER WHAT CIRCUMSTANCES SHOULD YOU SHOW CARDS?

Good question. Exposing cards can be a fine way to manipulate your foes. Showing big cards after big bets may train your enemies to fold to your bluffs. Likewise, showing the odd naked bluff could gain you a loose call later on. Trouble is, you never know exactly what sort of image you're going to need in ten minutes or half an hour; showing your bluffs, for example, may deny you bluffing opportunities later when you need them most. You also run the risk of giving real information to foes savvy enough to see through whatever smoke you're trying to blow.

Does this mean you should never show cards? Well, you

couldn't go far wrong with that choice. But to me, poker is a never-say-never game. I can think of a couple of cases where showing cards would be good even if it were your rarest exception. Can you?

>>

How about this? You're in a very loose and friendly game and want to give the impression of being loose and friendly, too. If others are showing cards, you might want to show a hand or two, too, just to join the party, so to speak. In such instances, show either your uncalled monsters or your straightforward wins. You'll give away the least real information, while seeming to be one of the gang.

In a larger sense, look to integrate your card-showing choices into your overall image. If you have a frisky image, say, and you're using it to run the table, you can easily reinforce it by showing all kinds of different hands. This will send the message that you'll bet with anything and raise with anything, and make it difficult for your lesser foes to figure out where you're at.

It's also possible that by showing cards that reveal nothing about your strategy, you might induce someone to give you something real about theirs. For instance, if I'm in the big blind with a junk hand and someone raises into me, I'll show them that 7-2 when I fold. Some of them will respond reflexively and show the small pocket pair or medium ace they saw fit to raise with. My information is worthless—*I fold crap hands*—but theirs may tell me something I didn't yet know.

In the main, I'll show cards when I'm a strong player in a weak game, and not show when I'm a weak player in a small game. But I try not to be dogmatic, and neither should you: If you *never* show cards, give yourself the homework assignment of showing some cards your next time out. Even circumspection can be a habit, and it never hurts to give all your habits a good, sound shake from time to time.

* * *

AFTER A CASH GAME BUSTOUT

Well, the good news is I don't have to waste time at the cashier's cage.

* * *

METHINKS THE LADDIE DOTH PROTEST TOO MUCH

Friends found me playing in the $100 buy in no limit game when there were $200 and $500 buy in games going on. They mocked me for playing so small, and I became defensive, trying to justify my choice in terms of game selection, long waiting lists, bankroll requirements, even feng shui. Know what? All those justifications were nonsense. Really, I was just defending my ego. I didn't want to seem small time. But the game I was in was soft, profitable, and beatable, and the other games were not. For this reason, I didn't have to justify myself to anyone. But even if I were playing small out of pure fear of playing higher, *I don't have to justify myself to anyone.* Neither do you. If you're making your own decisions according to your own best judgment, they're bound to look funky to others every now and then. Don't care about that. Just don't care at all. The opinions of others—even friends—don't matter nearly so much as getting yourself into the most favorable game situation you can find. That's just ego talking, and your ego's just noise. I've said it before and I'll say it again:

SAVE YOUR EGO FOR THE CASHIER'S CAGE.

That's the place it belongs.

* * *

ANOTHER GOOD THING ABOUT BREATHING IN

Skillful players know enough to challenge and test players just entering a game. They know that their foes might be not yet mentally prepared to get involved and can be counted on to make certain sorts of weak, loose, cally mistakes. But when you breathe in to the game, it neutralizes their effort to put pressure on you, since you're going to play your same insanely tight strategy whether they pressure you or not. Early in your session, when it's your goal to *get information*, not *get involved*, they actually do you a favor by trying to bully you, for they identify themselves as bullies, which information you can use against them later when the time is right.

* * *

A LINE I LIKE

If I'm fortunate enough to win the first couple of hands I play, I often say, "It will quickly become apparent to you that I'm only in the pot with a winning hand." Try that line, or a line like it. By verbally reinforcing your success, you create the impression that you routinely play strong hands strongly. This gives you the option of playing weak hands strongly as well.

* * *

SOMETHING ABOUT HORSES
AND MIDSTREAMS

When your plan for the hand is flop dependent, don't change your plan just because the flop doesn't come your way. Example: I'm in the big blind with A-K offsuit, facing a late position raise from a very tricky, very strong player. It's folded back to me. I could reraise, but I'm aware that if I miss the flop I may have to check-fold, for I won't be able to put this notoriously frisky player on a hand. So my plan for the hand is this: flat call, looking to hit an ace or a king on the flop, and trap. The flop, though, comes T-J-9. I check and my foe makes a pot size bet. If I call this bet, I will have changed my plan for the hand from "hit and trap" to "snap off a bluff." Now, that's a grand plan for a hand, but it's not the one I set out with here. Nor is a pure bluff likely here, since those middle cards are the ones that frisky players love to raise with. At minimum, he has to have a semi-bluff with some kind of draw. To call with only overcard and gutshot straight outs is to engage in a certain self-indulgent wishful thinking. Better to get away from this hand while the pot is still small than to get involved in a confrontation where I (probably) have to hit to win. The cumulative small surrenders will do less damage to my stack than the one big, rash, wrong choice, especially when that choice is motivated by the wishful thinking of having hit the flop. In all events, we have to see what is, not what we yearn for.

In a related story, if you need to hit the flop twice, don't stick around if you hit it just once. For instance, let's say you've made a package hand raise with 8-7 suited. Your plan for this hand was to win without a fight or, at most, to get one caller that you could CB off the pot on the flop. This time, though, you get no less than three callers. You know you're dominated—probably currently trailing the field. Now you're looking for a highly favorable flop like 7-8-2. This is not wishful thinking, it's adaptation. But here's the key: When the flop comes 7-K-2, you're done with the hand. Yes, you hit the flop, but you only hit it once, and your holding is squirrelly, to say the least. New plan: Minimize your damage and get away from this adventure as cheaply as possible.

It's no mistake to take a flier on a package hand, especially if you think you can fold the field. But it is a mistake to disregard the obvious information of all those calls and continue playing when you can't possibly be in great shape.

* * *

COUNTERINTUITIVE, BUT . . .

It's possible for a player to be risk affined and risk averse on the same hand. Many players, for example, will see fit to raise in early position with A-8, which is certainly a risk affined move. But then the flop comes K-K-5. Now, the ace might very well be the boss card—but then again, it may not, and many players will quickly turn risk averse in this circumstance, content to check it down if that possibility is on offer.

Can you think of times when you've gone from strong to weak in the play of a single hand?

>>

Here's another example. J-J raises his own big blind, gets several callers, and checks a flop of 6-6-4. Why check this flop? Pure risk aversion. An ace on the turn freezes him completely and kills his action. With those problematic pocket jacks, I'd have turned it around, taken a free look at the big blind and come out betting into the orphan flop. Sure, there might be an A-6 out there against me, but I also might get calls from A-4 or even just overcards.

* * *

THE LOGIC OF COMPLETING THE SMALL BLIND

If there are three or four limpers in front of you and a passive big blind behind you, you probably have odds to call with any old rags in the small blind. But have no illusions: Almost all the time, you will have wasted the cost of completion. And you can *only* allow yourself the luxury of this call if you have the self-knowledge and discipline to get away from your hand if you miss or, especially, only half hit.

* * *

DON'T BE PARANOID

When you've been stalled and card dead for a long time and come in for a raise only to face a reraise, it's easy to see monsters in the closet. It seems like they know you've been down and are now reraising you—*messing with you*—just to keep you down. While some foes are capable of this level of sophistication and torment, it's much more likely that, well, they just have raiseworthy hands. Probably they're not paying all that much attention to you anyhow, and have no thought at all about how you've been running. But subjective reality makes us see abusive moves that aren't there. Don't be paranoid. Your foes don't hate you or want to victimize you; most of the time they're just playing their hands.

*   *   *

FOUND OBJECT

Of a player who is—literally—sleeping through his blinds: "This guy gives the expression 'out button' a whole new meaning."

16

HOW I "WON" THE WORLD SERIES OF POKER

One thing we all know about poker—especially NLHE with its countless variables and situational considerations—is how hard it is to make the right choice in the moment, and how easy it is to second guess after. Taking that idea one step further, I have often found that my understanding of poker deepens if I create poker situations away from the table and mentally walk through them while I have the luxury of time to set them up, examine them at length from many different angles, and choose the path I consider correct. In a sense this is like watching poker unfold in slow motion. I find that it improves my ability to have a plan for the hand when I'm actually involved in the hand, and time is not an abundant luxury.

With that in mind, I'd like you to join me on the following flight of poker fantasy. I would encourage you also to construct such fantasies for yourself. They teach one to think creatively—and, as you will see, humbly—about the game.

Just for fun, I set this event in 2005, in the "new and improved" Binion's Horseshoe in downtown Las Vegas. Some will argue that a "new and improved Horseshoe" is on a par with a "new and improved holey sock." Others will note that in the "real world," the World Series of Poker was held in 2005 at the Rio Hotel and Casino. Call it artistic license or a fondness for old school, but in my universe, in this instance, I've left the World Series of Poker *in situ.*

Herewith, then, my fictional win at the World Series of Poker.

THE END OF THE BEGINNING

"It's simple you call me up," reads the lamentably punctuated promo card. "If you like I stay if not I simply go away no obligation." I turn the card over and gaze upon the picture of *Carmen, a actual entertainger.* Saying a silent prayer for crimes against usage, I open my hand and let the card flutter down to commingle with the ambient grit and flotsam of the Vegas pavement.

May, 2005. I'm standing in the middle of Fremont Street, Las Vegas, USA. A sirocco wind frisks in off the desert, giving a convection oven feel to the space beneath the curved and perforated roof of the Fremont Street Experience. Directly before me, the yawning maw of Harrah's Horseshoe offers the sweet promise of chill, air-conditioned air, but I'm not quite ready to go in yet. The main event of the World Series of Poker starts in ten minutes.

I am not ready yet.

When Harrah's bought Binion's Horseshoe Casino in early 2004, everyone thought that they'd strip mine its minimal assets and tear the relic down. Then the 2004 World Series of Poker came along and broke every attendance record in sight, with a final event field so gargantuan that they nearly ran out of tables, chairs, chips, dealers, decks of cards, floor space, patience, common sense, and oxygen. No way could they hold the tournament at the 'Shoe ever again, everyone said. Baby had outgrown the crib, and must necessarily be shifted to a larger, more accommodating space.

But Harrah's evidently figured that moving the WSOP from its hallowed home would render it just another nondescript stop on the endless tournament trail. Rather than divest the old gambling hall of its only real asset, they took a different approach. They gutted the main floor of the casino, nuked every single table game and slot machine, and converted the whole space into a poker room of vast and overwhelming proportion. They raised the ceilings, retooled the ventilation, and remodeled everything, including the lamentable bathrooms, which had long been the nearest thing to an indoor outhouse. Then they iced the cake by pimping the place with the sexiest, high-techiest gear they could find: tables with built-in shuffle machines; digital sign-up boards with satellite readouts throughout the cardroom; flat screen TVs for every conceivable line of sight; wholly holographic chips.

Smart money said they were nuts. Smart money said no way could a dedicated poker hall survive in Las Vegas, not where the average mook wants nothing more challenging from his gamble than dice to toss or slot reels to watch spin while he downs free drinks and fritters his pittance away. But when word got out about this place in Vegas . . . this pure poker environment unsullied by other gambles and undistracted by the bonk and clang of pull toys . . . well, Harrah's may have wondered if they'd thought too small. Players came and players stayed. In the upshot, the 'Shoe was reborn.

Meanwhile, back at my modest career, I happened to catch the eye of a new online poker site called pokerbeatsworking.com. Blessed with more startup cash than common sense, they hired me at extravagant sums of money to do not much more than grace their magazine ads with my smiling face. If you've ever seen my smiling face, you'll know it's graceless, and if you've ever seen me play poker, you'll know that, "as a poker player, I'm a pretty good writer." These blunt facts notwithstanding, the worthies at pokerbeatsworking decided to bankroll my entry into the 2005 World Series of Poker, the $10,000 main event, for which there are some 5,023 players taking their seats even as we speak.

Oh, and I'm wired, wired for sight and sound. Everything I

say or do during the tournament will be immediately uplinked and posted to the web. This—the prospect of having the world watch and critique and second-guess my every play—just squares and cubes the present gnarl in my stomach. If I make a fool of myself, everyone will know, and instantly. Whatever poker credibility I've ever managed to accrue could be squandered by one promiscuous call or stupid brain fart.

Good times.

But one thing I know about no limit Texas hold'em is that you must be unafraid to lose. You must be prepared to move your money, even when you know it could cost you everything. No problem for me on that score—hell, it's not my money. But also, you must be willing to look dumb, sometimes real dumb. Your reads and your reasoning will put you in situations where if things go right you'll seem like a genius, but if they go wrong you'll end up with a face full of idiot cream pie. People may laugh at you, disrespect or disdain you. Call you a donkey to your braying, dully protesting face. If you can't handle that, then NLHE, especially tournament hold'em, is not a game you can win.

So here I stand on the threshold of the resurrected 'Shoe, trying to calm my nerves, steady my hands, steel myself for the battle ahead. I glance down at the picture of *Carmen, a actual entertainger,* and wonder what she's doing right now. The main event of the 2005 World Series of Poker is about to start. Mustering what bravado I can, I swallow hard and waltz into the air-conditioned cool. "If you like I stay if not I simply go away no obligation."

A tournament strategy if there ever was one.

PAT HAND

The guy in the three seat thinks he's a wag. He wears a name tag that reads, "Hello, I'm Pat Hand," which I imagine he imagines is the height of hilarity. So far there's been nothing funny about his play. Recognizing me as that wired writer from that website, and the author of all those books, he's made it his mission to attack my blinds. Every time I fail to defend, he says, "Those who can't do, teach, huh, Mr. Writer Man? Huh? And you can't do *or* teach."

I'm not going to let him get under my skin, of course. My game plan for day one of the World Series of Poker in no way includes the strategy *let the loudmouth rattle you*. So I'm not rising to Pat Hand's bait—but I am going to school on his play, and looking for appropriate cards with which to counterattack.

Now, let's not confuse appropriate cards with top tickets. In NHLE, high cards can carry you only so far. If all you do is play big pairs and big paint, you become too predictable, too easy to read; you can't really trap because your strength is too easily deduced. So of every hand I'm dealt, I don't ask, "Does this hand meet my starting requirements?" but rather, "What's the best thing to do with these cards right now?" Very occasionally the best thing to do with pocket aces is muck 'em, and the best thing to do with 2-7 is move all in. With Pat Hand, I'm looking specifically for middle suited connectors, a holding with versatility and hidden strength . . . a hand I can use to break him.

First, though, I've gotta lull him into a false sense of stupidity, either by releasing my blinds outright when he raises, or else calling small raises and then check-folding on the flop. I want to train this guy to attack me, and I want him to think he can do it all he wants.

Next, I start getting a little verbally fidgety. I'm a pretty good actor—it's a strength of my game—and I persuasively sell my annoyed response to his relentless pressure. This, of course, just encourages him to hit harder. He's having the time of his life, too, pushing me around for all the (cyber)world to see. He's even phoning friends and telling them to check out my feed. While my clients at pokerbeatsworking.com might appreciate the extra traffic, I'm more interested in Pat Hand's starting requirements. They're starting to soften, and soon he'll be raising with nothing.

Comes a deal when he makes his standard raise into my blind, and I make my standard call. I've got 9♦-8♦, my weapon of choice, and the flop couldn't be much more favorable: 9♣-6♦-5♥. I've got top pair, a gutshot straight draw, and a backdoor flush draw. I've also got a foe who, thanks to his rising incaution, can now be counted on to have not much of a hand at all. I put him on something like K-J.

He makes a pot sized bet, expecting me to do what I've done every time: whinge and whinge and fold. This time, though, I whinge and whinge and . . . call. He cocks an eyebrow and says, "That's the most aggressive call I've seen all day." I don't reply, but I'm sure he interprets my action as, *I'm tired of you pushing me around and I want to play back at you—but I'm too scared to play back strong.*

The turn card is the 9♥ and now I figure I'm bulletproof. He could conceivably be on a better nine than mine, but that's just one of a wide range of hands I've trained him to get involved with. I've expanded the chances, in other words, of him having a hand other than the one he needs to have right now.

I check. He bets. I visibly wince . . . .and then raise the minimum. The wince and raise together should come off as either a clumsy attempt to disguise the real power of my hand or else a clumsy stab at playing back at him without risking too many of my chips. The trouble for Pat is that these interpretations fight against each other. He can't know whether I'm strong-faking-weak or weak-faking-strong. And since I've got him getting involved with inferior values, he's probably out ahead of his hand. If he's on overcards, he can only win with a bluff, and then only if I'm on the weak-faking-strong side of the ledger.

For success in NLHE generally, you want to be the one who knows, not the one who guesses. This mostly means being the bettor, not the caller. Occasionally, though, if you've set your trap right, you can get your foe raising on a guess—especially when his judgment is colored by ego. Right now, Pat has a frothing need to cripple or bust or outplay "Mr. Writer Man," so he comes down on the side of *raise* and pushes in his stack. I call and we table our hands. He's got K-T, and his face falls when he sees my nine. The river's a rag and I double through.

A few hands later, Pat Hand is eliminated when he puts his short stack in with some egregious cheese and gets called in five places.

This skirmish tells me two things about my play today: that my perception is crisp, and that my image is working. Armed with these two tools, I go on to finish day one of the WSOP with about 50,000 in chips. It's nowhere near the lead, but at least I'm still in the hunt. Score one for "Mr. Writer Man." We go to tomorrow.

KNOCKIN' ON HEAVEN'S DOOR

My wife once told me, "Don't mix apples with ducks."

"Don't you mean apples with oranges?" I asked.

"Nah," she answered, "you can mix those all you want. But if you're mixing apples and ducks, then you're really working at cross-purposes to yourself."

Sadly, this is just the bind I find myself in midway through play on day two. On the apple hand, I'm trying to play great poker, win-the-whole-shooting-match poker. On the duck hand, though, I know that some hundreds of poker fans an hour (the number started small but the back office tells me it's growing) are now looking over my cyber-shoulder as I play. All of my moves, especially yesterday's amputation of Mr. Pat Hand, are being discussed and dissected at length in the chat rooms of pokerbeatsworking and elsewhere. Some think I'm playing well. Some think I'm just butt-lucky. I shouldn't care what anyone thinks. I should just play my game. But I do care. Finding myself with fans, of all the improbable things, I discover that I don't want to disappoint them by busting out today.

Apple, meet duck.

I have become cautious, tentative, and conflicted, and in this state of confusion have managed to grind 50,000 in chips down to about 16K. This is not where I want to be. Nowhere near where I want to be. My goal for the day was to finish around a hundred grand, but my first job now is just to stop the bleeding caused by my own cowering cowardice, or at the end of play today the only place I'll be is in some internet chat room, trying to explain why I played like such a pumpkin.

So it happens that around midday I try to reverse my Timmy trend with, unfortunately, a reckless adventure involving a middle pocket pair. Having raised preflop and bet into a seemingly safe flop, I have had to fold in the face of a big reraise. My cowering cowardice rises like gorge in my throat. Now, alas, I am seriously imperiled. The blinds are 400 and 800, and the antes 150. With my stack at just over 10K, I'm not dead yet, but definitely knocking on heaven's door. In all likelihood, I'm heading for a make-or-break moment.

It's upon me sooner than I think.

I pick up pocket jacks in middle position. Those damn jacks. Since no one has opened the pot before it gets to me, I'm clearly not going to fold. Should I push all in or just call and hope to flop a set? It's a measure of my indecision that I make the weeniest move possible, doubling the blind to make a minimum raise.

Now you have to understand I'm looking over my own shoulder, too. Like the folks back home, I'm second-guessing my every move. Whatever concentration or clarity of purpose I may have had yesterday is just a memory now. I am, truly, a cork bobbing on the sea of poker.

Which the player on the button must sense. He raises me back 2,400. This is a perfect bet, because it compounds the error of my neither-here-nor-there opening raise. If I call, I'm probably pot committed, and if I raise all in I could very well be pushing my chips into a bigger pocket pair. The least of these evils is to fold like an origami crane, and this, I expect, is what the button expects me to do. Why wouldn't I? I'm so clearly playing not to lose right now that . . . that . . .

That he's counting on me to be not willing to put my tournament life on the line!

Which means he doesn't want me to call.

Which means he's making a move.

Should I call him and get him to bluff me all in on the flop? That way lies madness. Any ace, king, or queen on the flop and I'll have to let the hand go. No, the time to go big or go home is right now. And if that means the end of my World Series, so be it. You've got to be not afraid to lose, and not afraid to look foolish. If he's on a bigger pocket pair, I'll definitely look foolish and likely bust out. Even if he's got two overcards, it's a coin flip, and I hate, hate, *hate* the coin flip.

But I don't think that's where he's at. I think he's pushing me around. I've certainly painted myself as pushable, have I not?

So, "All in," I croak, and push my chips forward. There they go. All the apples. All the ducks.

He thinks for not very long, calls, and turns over A-7 suited, a better (and by better, of course, I mean worse) hand than I could have hoped for. I'm about a 2–1 favorite to win, and when my hand holds up, I kick heaven's door closed for now.

I dodged a bullet. Believe me, I know the caliber and lethality of the bullet I just dodged. Somehow this clears my head. All the confusion melts away, replaced by a *screw it* attitude that says be in it to win it. Armed with this attitude, I proceed to reel off a string of strong plays, and finish day two at 100K. Just exactly where I wanted to be.

There'll be a lot of internet chat tonight. I'll have my supporters and detractors, but now I know to put them out of my mind. This is my tournament, not theirs, and no matter how vested their interest, it ain't nearly so vested as mine. I played today for the fans, and it nearly did me in. Tomorrow—and for days after, one hopes—I'm going to be playing for me.

And if I lose, believe me, I'll be disappointed enough for us all.

TV TABLE

Midway through play on day three, with the starting field of 5,000+ having been whittled to a "modest" 700 or 800 players, I'm lifted and shifted to the TV table. I assume this is luck of the draw, and has nothing to do with my stunning good looks (absent) or my dazzling strategy (get lucky).

In any case, there I am, awkwardly essaying the trick of showing my hole cards to the embedded little lipstick cam while ESPN's other cameras swoop and hover like carrion eager to feast on the—let's face it, agony of defeat makes great television—bustouts. I'm determined not to be one of these, and seem to be in no immediate danger, for my chip count is up over 150K; not the chip lead, yet not chopped liver.

Twentysomething wunderkind Roger "Run the Table" Sable is sitting to my immediate left. He's living up to his nickname, banging away at pot after pot, hardly letting anyone else get a bet in edgewise. Not what you'd call a camera shy guy, he's also milking his moment at the TV table with jokes, banter, and frequent forays to the rail to swap spit with his pneumatic gal pal.

With Sable on my left, my first thought is to just sit tight and hope for big tickets. Yeah, that's the safe strategy, but it's not the game I came to play. Having crossed my Rubicon of doubt on day two, I'm looking to put myself in a position to win this thing, and letting Sable stall me out for hours is not going to advance that cause.

I'm going to have to get creative.

I cast my mind back to my joust with Pat Hand. By painting myself as weak, loose, and tilty, I seduced him into betting off all his chips with a lock loser. But that clown had all the mental deftness of a dinosaur egg. Sable's going to be a much trickier safe to crack, especially since he's got position.

But hang on now, maybe I can use his positional advantage against him. After all, he knows he's got position, plus table image, lots of chips, and a fierce reputation. All of these things can be expected to keep a player like me in line. And what does a player like me, thus kept in line, do? He sits tight and hopes for big tickets.

Since Sable takes this as my default strategy, I figure I'm probably clear to run at least one check-raise bluff. I wait long enough to look tight, then limp into a pot in middle position with rags. When Roger makes his standard, probing, *let's see what you're made of, shoe clerk,* raise, I reraise him a third of my stack. As expected, he puts me on the big-ticket tip and gets away from his hand. That's a pot, but that's only part A.

Now he's alert to the possibility that the guy in front of him is not a complete rollover. He's wondering whether I had a hand back there or just a questing spirit. A little while later, I flat call his under the gun raise from my big blind, then check-raise a flop so ragged he has to figure me for a piece of it. When he folds, that's part B.

You know the expression, "Third time's the charm"? Well, around here we say, "Third time's the adjustment." When you run a series of moves on someone, your first shot comes as a surprise, and as a surprise it usually works. Your second stab in the same direction provokes great suspicion: Just as two points define a line, two frisky moves (such as check-raises) suggest a trend toward treachery. A foe of sufficient cleverness can detect these trends and unscramble their patterns. Then . . . *third time's the adjustment.* The third time you try your move, your enemy is ready to pounce. The first time I reraised, Sable became alert. The second time I reraised, he formed a hypothesis. On my third reraise he'll know I'm a lying sack of cheese, and come after me. This would be part C.

Everyone knows you don't win big tournaments without

some breaks along the way. These breaks are commonly thought of as, you know, your pocket pair holding up against A-K, or an underdog draw that gets there. To me, the luck of poker is something slightly different. It's getting the cards you need in order to sell what you're selling when the market is hot. I'd set up Sable to believe that I wasn't going to let him by golly run the table. He thinks I've stuck a neck in a noose and now he's ready to hang me. Next time I flat call, he'll raise with any semi-strong hand and if I reraise—which he expects I'll do according to the program he thinks I'm running—he'll come over the top for a massive bet and put my feet to the fire.

Luck, then, is me picking up pocket kings while this idea is still fresh in his mind. Luck is Sable deciding that pocket jacks—those problematic jacks—is a sufficiently strong hand with which to launch his counterattack. Luck isn't really kings holding up over jacks; that'll happen eight times out of ten, more or less. Had I sat tight and waited for big tickets, I'd have taken a small piece of Walter on that hand. By setting up and defeating his expectation, I'm able to grab most of his chips.

Now I'm the big stack at the TV table, and now I get to play bully. For two solid hours, no one else can get a raise in edgewise, and I run my stack up to almost half a million. Somewhere along the way we burst the money bubble and cross into payday. I hardly even notice. A mere money finish no longer interests me. My engine is hitting on all cylinders now, and if she doesn't throw a piston rod, she might go all the way.

MONEY SHOT

Another day, another adrenaline shot to the heart.

Inspired by yesterday's surgical dismantling of Roger Sable, I have gone on to build my chip total up over three million. That seems like a mound—and it is—but at the final table an average chip stack will be north of five million, so I've still got some work to do.

Part of my job is straightforward: Attack the short stacks. Since so many stacks are short relative to mine, I've got lots of targets to shoot at. So I'm opening lots of pots for raises, then betting any flop that looks the least bit orphaned. If they call on the flop, I put them all in on the turn. Once I show my willingness to fire both barrels, I get many laydowns and win lots of blinds and antes. It's a modestly profitable stack building exercise, but it's not what I'm looking for.

I'm looking for the money shot.

See, conventional wisdom says that big stacks should avoid confrontations with other big stacks. But I have no intention of coasting to the final table. I want to take it by towering storm, and for that to happen I'm going to have to double through something sizeable, and still keep building from there.

Eventually my table breaks and I'm moved to the charming proximity of Gwendolyn Brattle, the young U.K. pro who recently raised eyebrows (and whatnot) by gracing the pages of *Playboy*. Used to be she could use her stunning looks to gull her male opponents into nimrod moves, but no more. She's a known quantity now. Known mostly for her fiercely aggressive approach to (as she listed it under *turn-ons* in the text accompanying her *Playboy* pictorial) "ironing out the slackjaws."

Like me, she's got about three million in chips, and with Gwen in the two seat and me in seat seven, we're perfectly placed to take turns bullying the lesser stacks off their hands. By tacitly agreeing to steer clear of each other, we could carve up the table like Spain and Portugal once carved up South America. And for a while, I let her think that's the way it's going to be.

A situation like this actually gives big stacks greater power to bluff one another. The assumption is that if a big stack goes after another big stack, especially when easy pickings abound, there must be a big hand motivating the move. You can win a lot of chips this way. But you can never bust another player on a bluff, and I'm looking to bust Gwen now, so I turn up the heat, reraising her raises and blowing her off her hands.

She gives me this glare like, *Don't you know what we're supposed to be doing here?* I smile blankly. And put on my headphones. Crank up the reggae. Spain has broken off negotiations with Portugal. Portugal is on her own.

This brings Gwen to a crossroads. She can either shut down and concede control of the table, or else start popping me back when I reraise. Since her reputation precedes her, I know she'll have trouble turning turtle. It's just not in her nature, and it's a fact of life, or at least of poker, that people stay true to their nature. I've got her primed to make resteal raises, and if I happen to have a hand once when that happens, well . . . after that we'll let the cards decide. Like I said, I'm not coasting to the final table.

And you can call it lucky, if you like, that I again catch the right hand at the right time—but didn't I create the right time through a series of moves extending back through the match? First I've pushed Gwen off the notion that we're in cahoots. Then I yielded to a resteal move or two to embolden her. Now she's raising in middle position and I'm reraising from the button. Here comes her resteal reraise. I don't entirely disrespect the move. She has, after all, committed more than half her stack, and I know she wouldn't do that with just nothing. Nevertheless, I come over the top.

She doesn't like it . . . feels she may have been trapped . . . but if she releases she'll be imperiled, just another lesser stack at the mercy of my chips. Better, she decides, to make her stand right now. She calls all in and tables her hand. A♥-K♥.

But I have A-A.

I know in this matchup I'll win nine times out of 10, but I still hold my breath until my hand holds up. The dealer shoves me her chips. (And three million in chips takes some shoving.)

I have accomplished my goal. I'll go to the final table with a dominant chip lead. When I get there, well, I like ironing out slackjaws, too.

LAST SLACKJAW STANDING

Unwinding in my hotel room last night I happened to catch an old poker broadcast on TV. You know that famous one where world class poker pro Joey Colson seemingly inadvertently knocks a bunch of his chips into the pot? Despite Colson's protests, the tournament director rules that the bet must stand. Colson's foe, sensing weakness, moves all in. Colson calls—and turns over pocket aces. There's been great debate in the poker community about whether Colson's move was an act, an accident, or an angle shot. Colson said it was a mistake.

I say players of Colson's caliber don't make mistakes.

No, that's what players of my caliber do.

It sometimes happens, though, that players of his caliber and my caliber meet; thus today when we find ourselves heads up at the final table of the World Series of Poker's main event. Between us we have eliminated the other eight players, and have for the past two hours traded blinds, feints, and noncommittal pot steals. At this point I have a tiny chip lead, just north of 25 million in chips. Colson, though, whose ego is as legendary as his poker skill, probably still figures himself to be the favorite, and (legendary ego notwithstanding) probably he's right. After all, he's been here many, many times before, and he has the bracelets to prove it. Me, I've won as many major poker titles as Kermit the Frog. I think Colson's surprised I've lasted this long.

Antes at this point are 200,000, with blinds of 500,000 and one million. Picking up pocket deuces in the small blind, I allow a frisky idea to form in my mind, for it suddenly occurs to me that against Colson, though probably against no one

else, I can make these deuces look like aces. I fumble a bet of
about seven million over the betting line into the pot—and
then try to pull half of it back.

Colson's eyes narrow, and I know what he's thinking: How
dare a lowly *scribe* try to poach a play from his playbook? He
calls for the tournament director, who naturally and correctly
rules my seven million in play. This is just what I want, for
against pocket aces the best hand you can hold (beside the
other two aces) is 7-8 suited. But you're still better than a 3–1
dog, and Colson knows this. I figure he'll fold, I'll pick up his
blind, and we'll move on, because of course he can't call.

He calls.

Crikey.

While the dealer prepares to burn and turn I hotly recrimi-
nate myself for launching such a stupid reckless adventure.
Trying to fool Colson with his own gag? He saw right through
that. He read me like a book. Like the book *What Kind of Putz
Am I?*

But the flop comes 7-8-2, and I've hit a set. Having cracked
my code ("aces = not-aces") Colson will now definitely try to
bet me off my random hand. When he does, I'll come over the
top for all my chips. If he calls, I'll win! *I'll be the last slackjaw
standing!* All he has to do is bet.

Colson checks.

*He checks?! He can't possibly check here. Unless he bought my
aces act after all. But if he did, why would he have called preflop?
Could it be . . . ?* Ego! Colson's legendary ego. Having seen me
use his own trick in a sincerest-form-of-flattery way, he has
now risen to the bait in a manner I hadn't expected. Even ced-
ing a 3–1 advantage, he figures he can outplay me given the
facts that A) he knows what I hold and B) he's him and I'm
me.

So why the fuck did he check?!

Because he's trapping. He's got 7-8 suited and he's just
flopped two pair and he's trapping. He's checked so that I can
bet so that *he* can come over the top. *Bingo!* Now all I have to

do is step into his trap, let him spring it, and spring mine back.

So why the fuck do I check?!

I wish I could tell you. I can see the whole thing laid out in my mind. I *know* it will work. But some old poker programming deep inside me yells, *You've got a monster. Check!* So I do.

And the flop comes another eight. *Dios mio!* Joey Colson has the nut full house. In a second he's going to bet, and I'm going to fold, and that will be that. I have the dark feeling that this is my high water mark. I've shot my wad. From this point forward, Colson's skill will edge me out and I'll finish a respectable but disappointing second. I won't be the last slack-jaw standing after all. Here at the beginning of the end, I wait for Colson to bet.

But he checks again!

Now what is he thinking? That I'll view the eight as a safe card and go ahead and bet my aces at last? He must be wondering why I didn't bet them on the flop. Maybe he's decided that I don't have aces after all, that I have something like A-K suited, and the only way he can get more money in the pot is to let me bluff at it.

Like I'm going to do that. I check.

The river card comes. Colson can't check now: I've checked the flop and the turn; he can't expect me to do his betting for him. So he goes ahead and makes a pot sized bet.

What the hell, I think, *if you're doing something and you can't stop doing it, keep on doing it.* I don't say, "All in," but I do push all my chips over the line.

Then I try to pull half of them back.

Colson comes out of his chair! All his cool disappears in an instant as he shouts—*shouts*—at the tournament director to make my bet stand. The TD gives me this look like, *How did a chump like you make the final two?* Then, for the second time in the hand, he rules that my full bet must play.

Colson calls in a heartbeat. We table our hands. 8-7 for Colson. And for me? Well, the river was a deuce.

You do the math. The odds against catching your miracle one-outer are fortysomething to one. You'll get there roughly 2 percent of the time. But really, you only have to get there once.

All week long in this tournament I've set up situations where if I happened to catch the right kind of hand at the right time I could cripple a foe. I've been able to couple some (with all due false modesty) fairly clever play with some fairly fortuitous cardfalls. This one time—the time I needed it most— a brilliantly fortuitous cardfall saved me from my own dull blunders and won me a title. It's just luck, and I know it's just luck, but no one wins these things without luck, so all I'm really doing is taking my place at the end of a long line of lucky people who've won.

I go off to celebrate. I'm happy in a way I've never been happy before. The money is great, of course; the money is overwhelming. But what I really like is that I've made my bones as a player. No longer just Mr. Writer Guy, I'm now Mr. Writer Guy with a bracelet, though the thought occurs to me that I'll have to come back next year and defend. That's a sobering thought, the kind that keeps you awake nights.

It's enough to make a man quit playing poker for good.

But I suspect it probably won't.

17

THE LAST WORD

Would you be shocked to learn that I'm playing poker online while I'm writing these words? You shouldn't be. During the writing of this book I've probably spent as much time not writing it as writing it, if you take my meaning. Every time I've gotten stuck for a word, or reached the end of a chapter, or the end of a page, or just the bottom of my coffee cup, I've bipped over to the internet for a few hands of the game I love, no limit Texas hold'em. It's wrought havoc with my productivity, I can tell you that, and I don't recommend the approach, either to writers or to poker players, for each distracts from the other as surely as my dog distracts me when he nudges my typing (or betting) hand with his nose. But, "Do as I say, not as I do," right? I've tried in this book to give you some good guidance on no limit Texas hold'em, and I've also tried to be frank and candid about where, when, and how I fail to heed my own advice.

Being frank and candid . . . that's a useful thing. No matter where you are in your development as a poker player—whether you're just starting out, just hitting your stride, or just hitting it big—being frank and candid is always a good idea. Your honesty, your pure, sheer honesty, will get you out of more poker traps than I can name. I'll bet you can name some, though, and since I've asked you to participate in this book all along, why would I start stopping now?

>>

Being frank and candid and all, I have no trouble admitting that poker really geeks me out. I'm a little astounded that after all the poker I've played and all the poker I've written about and discussed to death, the game still turns me on. You'd think I'd get tired of it eventually, but I haven't, not yet. I have no limit Texas hold'em to thank for this, for the game, with its infinite variety and mystery, has definitely reignited my passion for poker over the last couple of years. Not, frankly, that my passion was in that much danger of dying out. But there are just so many things about NLHE that get me off.

- Reraising all in against a foe I know is bluffing and watching him squirm
- Taking a draw with correct odds and getting there
- Bluffing with nothing and getting them to fold
- Making them fear me
- Figuring it all out; seeing the winning path through the hand

What gets you off about this game? Don't be shy—frank and candid, remember?

>>

Much as I love NLHE, I don't imagine for a second that I've gotten it solved. So I've weighed and measured, and endlessly second-guessed every concept I've presented to you here. I feel confident that my approach to the game is right—and equally confident that there are other, equally right, approaches out there. "The ocean is blue, but it's also wet," yeah? I've done my best to let my experience of the game illuminate yours. I've tried to shine a light from a certain point of view, but there are other lights and other points of view. So keep reading, keep studying, keep learning the game. No two paths of poker are even remotely alike, and serious students of the game are at least as interested in finding their own unique path as they are in winning lots of pots. You'll find your path if you look for it: in books and in your own notebook, where all your great discoveries lie. Mostly you'll find it at the table, in your long hours of play, and then away from the table as you mull why you did what you did and ask yourself how you could do better. But know (as I'm sure you do) that you'll never fully solve this game, for no limit hold'em is the ultimate funhouse expedition: Behind each new door lies another door.

I hope you'll take that idea on board, and I hope that every time you make a discovery about this wonderful game, you'll treat it as a launching pad to other discoveries. You'll find that they're there, and always will be. Remember how it was when you first discovered orphan flops, or phantom outs, or pressuring the bubble boys? These discoveries never stop coming, and there are new, unknown, exciting ones waiting just over the horizon.

For myself, I have an exciting new discovery of my own in store. The next Killer Poker book I write (and I'll probably start on it tomorrow, 'cause you know me and the addictive personality) will be a radical departure, a "how-to whodunit" combining elements of murder mystery and teaching tool. It's going to be called *Killer Poker: This Game Is Murder*, and I have every confidence that you'll enjoy it.

If, that is, I can tear myself away from the tables long enough to write it.

Glossary

BFM. Big fat middle; the heart of a successful, strategically planned cash game session.

Big Maxx. The K and Q of clubs.

Breathe in. To get acquainted with a new game and a new table by playing few hands and watching the action closely.

Bubble off. To finish one place out of the money.

Coming out hand. See *debutante hand*.

Complication raise. A raise made with a substandard hand in order to complicate your opponents' image of you.

Continuation bet. The postflop bet made by the preflop raiser; CB.

Crazy Ivan. See *faux rockets*.

Debutante hand. The first hand you play as you transition into the BFM.

Double infinity. Pocket eights.

Endorphin shock. The buzz of big bet poker.

Faux rockets. For bluffing purposes, hands preselected to be played as if they were pocket aces.

Flopportunity. A flop favorable to the hand you plan to represent.

Fold equity. The extra value in your bet derived from the possibility that everyone else might fold.

Foreclosure raise. A raise made by a drawing hand on the flop for the purpose of foreclosing the action and getting a free card on the turn.

FNL. Fast 'n' loose.

Franklin. AKA Big Ben; a hundred-dollar bill.

Fuckaroundarama. A loose, careless poker game, or the wild first hour of a low buy in, multiple rebuy tournament.

Fundraiser. Someone who habitually raises preflop, only to surrender the hand on the flop, thus raising funds for others.

Go off. To lose a lot of money through bad play, as in "to go off for a big number."

Hoover. A small bet from a strong hand designed to suck in callers.

Image equity. The value of how you're perceived in terms of the freedom you have to act.

Inner image. How you feel about your own play.

Jackthree. Junk; any unplayable hand.

Kosher. Standard play or player.

Last float on the clueless parade. The worst player at a table full of bad players.

Limpfest. When the majority of players in the hand limp in preflop; aka *limpede*.

LPOP. Little pair out of position.

LR. Lightning rod; someone whose presence has an inordinate effect on the game.

Min bet. The smallest legal bet or raise.

Min/max. A buy in condition for no limit cash games where the buy in is an exactly mandated amount.

Mirplo. See *nimrod*.

Money bubble. aka *bubble*—the final place of finish before tournament payouts begin.

Nimrod. See *pumpkin*.

OMHS. One More Hand Syndrome; the thing that keeps a poker player in a poker game; aka *chair glue*.

Oxygen-debt stupidity. Another reason players stay in games long after they should retire from the field.

Package hands. Sub-premium holdings, such as 7-8 suited, added into the normal "package" of raising hands.

Phantom outs. Cards that don't make a hand but do create bluffing opportunities; e.g., a third flush card.

Program. A predetermined betting sequence, such as check-calling on the flop and check-raising on the turn.

Pumpkin. A bad player.

Real estate raise. A raise made in late position, solely to exploit late position.

Rebuy fever. A willingness to gamble, even in unfavorable situations, during the rebuy phase of a tournament.

ROI. Return on investment; a way of expressing the relationship between card odds and pot odds.

RWC. Raise with cheese; a naked bluff with bad cards.

Timmy. Timid Timmy; a weak or cautious player.

Top/top. Top pair, top kicker.

True value. A straightforward, unimaginative player.

Tweener pair. A hand that competes against, and has a big edge over, an up-down holding; for example, 8-8 against A-5.

UTG. Under the gun; first to act after the blinds.

Wally. Cally Wally, a loose, weak player.

Wheelhouse. Any cards ten through ace.

Whiff. A flop that misses your hand completely.

Whinge. To whine or complain.

NOTES

This space intentionally left blank. Please intentionally fill.

_____

_____

_____

_____

_____

_____

_____

_____

_____

_____

_____

_____

_____

_____

_____

NOTES

NOTES

NOTES

About the Author

John Vorhaus has been writing about poker since 1988. His first book, *The Pro Poker Playbook*, is now a hard-to-find classic, but in recent years his prolific pen has yielded *Killer Poker: Strategy and Tactics for Winning Poker Play, Killer Poker Online: Crushing the Internet Game, The Killer Poker Hold'em Handbook, Killer Poker Online/2*, and *Poker Night: Winning at Home, in Casinos, and Beyond*.

When not writing about poker or playing poker, Vorhaus writes screenplays and television shows, and travels extensively teaching others how to do these things. His seminal writing books, *The Comic Toolbox* and *Creativity Rules!*, have guided and informed writers worldwide. His approach to the game of poker is summed up by the motto of his *Killer Poker* series: "Go big or go home!" He resides online at www.vorza.com